Android Application Development using Kotlin

(Build a Digital Note App from Scratch)

Stage-by-stage explanation of how the app was developed from start to finish

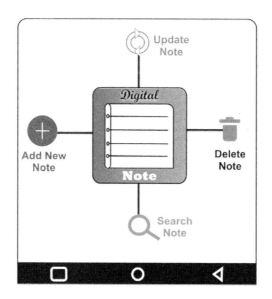

Featuring:

Kotlin | Android Studio 4.2 | View Binding | Room Database | LiveData | ViewModel | RecyclerView | Kotlin Coroutines | Bottom Navigation Bar | Settings Preferences | App Localization | Version Control with Git | App icon

JOSEPH AJIRELOJA

Android Application Development using Kotlin (Build a Digital Note App from Scratch):
Stage-by-stage explanation of how the app was developed from start to finish

Copyright © 2022. Joseph Ajireloja

Conceptualization, Design and Typesetting:

Joseph Ajireloja

First Edition

Published: February 2022.

ISBN: 9798419034846

Imprint: Independently published.

DEDICATION

This book is dedicated to Almighty God for His great love, grace, and goodness from the beginning of my life to this present moment and forever more; and also, to my caring and wonderful parents, Mr. and Mrs. I. O. Ajireloja and my marvelous siblings.

ACKNOWLEDGEMENTS

First and foremost, I give all the glory to God for helping me in the development of the mobile application, the writing of this book, and for everything.

Also, my appreciation goes to Google, Andela and Pluralsight for the learning opportunity and the wonderful support provided during my participation in Google Africa Developer Scholarship (GADS) 2021. It was a very nice experience.

Furthermore, my profound gratitude goes to my brother, Moses Ajireloja, for his support and help in proofreading this book, app testing and review, and French language translation added at the stage of app localization.

ABOUT THE AUTHOR

Joseph Ajireloja is a Software Developer, and an expert in Agricultural Extension and Rural Development. He is also a freelance Data Analyst and Graphic Designer. He has more than 7 years of experience in promoting computer proficiency and educating people on various computer-related or ICT skills.

Joseph obtained Diploma in Computer Science (Distinction), and holds a Bachelor of Agriculture (B.Agric.) degree in Agricultural Extension and Rural Development. He also holds a Master of Philosophy (M.Phil.) in Agricultural Extension and Rural Sociology, and currently studying for his Ph.D. degree in Agriculture and Rural Development.

He was a participant in the Google Africa Developer Scholarship (GADS) 2021, through which he learned and developed his knowledge and skills in Android Application Development using Kotlin Programming Language.

He is passionate about making positive impacts in the society and contributing his quota in helping people especially those in rural communities to improve their livelihoods and standard of living.

Author's e-mail: ajirelojajk@gmail.com

TABLE OF CONTENTS

CONTENT   **PAGE**

INTRODUCTION

In this book, you will learn about the processes and practical steps involved in Android Application Development lifecycle, using a case of "Digital Note". "Digital Note" is an android mobile application that can be used to take notes and save important records or plans.

"Digital Note" is available on Google Play Store. You can check it out and download it directly from Play Store (at https://bit.ly/digital-note-app) to have a full idea of what we will be building in this book.

I developed the application in Android Studio 4.2 using Kotlin programming language; so, we will also be using Kotlin in Android Studio in this book.

The contents of this book have been categorized into Stages for simplicity. A total of 31 stages make up this book.

In some of the lines of codes, I have included comments to provide more information about what the codes do. In the .xml files, comments are contained in **<!--   -->** (for example **<!-- Comments are here -->**, while in .kt files, lines of comments are preceded by **//** or enclosed within **/*   */** (for example, **// Here is my comment** or **/* Comments are here */**). *The complier will ignore any text or code that has been commented out and will not run it.*

NOTE: *To comment a line or multiple lines of code, simply highlight the line(s) of code and then press Ctrl + /.*

By the end of your study of this book, you should have gained good practical understanding of some important concepts in Android application development and, you should have developed a mobile app (with awesome user interface and features) that could create, read, update and delete data from Room Database.

We've got a lot to learn, so, let's get started.

STAGE 1
Planning and Design

At this stage, we will reflect on:

- the aim of developing the app or what the app should accomplish;
- how the app should look (that is, the user interface);
- the features and functionalities the app should have;
- who the potential users of the app are;
- the preparation of the resources (such as logo, images, contents, etc.) needed in the app.

Aim of developing the app

In the case of "Digital Note", our aim is to store or save notes and important records on our Android mobile phone or device without the need for internet connection.

In most cases, the aim or objectives of an app will be made known to you by your client- that is, the person or company or organization that contacted you to develop the app for them.

The aim of the app will guide you in choosing a name for it. It is advisable to have an app name that is not too long. App name with just one or two or three words should be cool.

How the app should look like

This has to do with the user interface (UI) of the app. *A very good UI has the possibility to draw potential users to download and use your app. You could consider learning about Material Design (learn more at https://material.io).*

However, in the case of "Digital Note", I already have some knowledge on Graphic Design using CorelDraw; so, I simply got the sketches for each of our desired screen (with their contents) done on plain sheet of paper using pencil and pen, and then launched CorelDraw to get the design done.

So, here is the simple design of the app done with CorelDraw:

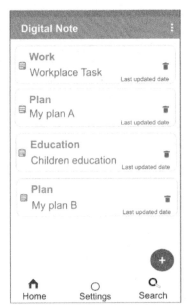

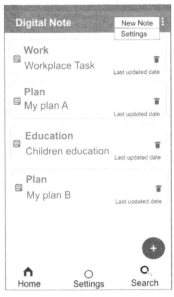

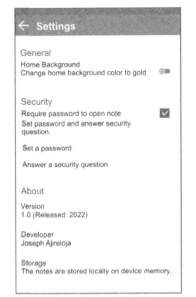

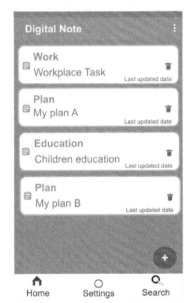

App features and functionalities

This has to do with how the app should function and what you will like it to do for you. In the case of "Digital Note", we would like to have features for adding new note with a category, title and details. Also, we would like to be able to modify or update notes, delete the notes that are no longer needed and, search for notes.

So, the "Digital Note" will have functionalities for inserting data to a database, updating the data in the database, deleting data from the database, and retrieving data from the database. In addition, the app will have Settings functionality from which we can change the home screen background colour from white to gold-related colour, and enable security password.

In most cases, the features or functionalities expected in a particular app will be described to you by your client.

Potential users

We need to think about the people that would possibly use the app, their geographical location, age range, language and culture.

You can consider localizing your app to support different languages so as to reach more potential users, particularly where English is not one of their common languages.

In the case of "Digital Note", all adults are the potential users. We will localize the app in French language to demonstrate how localization could be done.

Preparation of the resources needed in the app

It is important to itemize the resources (such as app logo icon, images, texts, translations and so on) that will be needed in developing the mobile app, and ensure that they are made available earlier so as not to slow than the app development process. In the case of "Digital Note", the app design, app logo, and wordings or texts (that is, string items) were well prepared.

STAGE 2
Android Studio Environment Setup

At this stage we will be setting up the Android Studio environment for the development of the application (that is, "Digital Note").

It is expected that you already have Android Studio installed on your computer system.

If you have not yet installed Android Studio, you can visit: https://developer.android.com/studio to download it. The latest version of Android Studio as of January 2022 is 2020.3.1.

However, since the version we will be using in this book is version 4.2.0, I encourage you to download Android Studio 4.2.0 released on May 4, 2021 directly from https://developer.android.com/studio/archive (Click on the button at the lower part of the page to agree to the terms on the page, so as to be able to navigate to the archive page where the different versions can be found).

Please note that part of the system requirements for Android Studio is a RAM of 8GB minimum, 64-bit OS, among others. Check out the system requirements located towards the bottom of the Android studio webpage. So, if your computer system has just 4GB RAM, you can consider upgrading it to 8GB so as to make the Android Studio and Emulator work seamlessly without slow-down or lag.

Also note that if you are installing and launching the Android Studio for the first time, you will need to be connected to the internet; this is because Android Studio will have to download some of its essential components online. The whole process might take about 30 minutes, depending on the speed of your internet. In subsequent launches of the software (after the first successful launch), internet is not required.

Now, let us launch our Android Studio (as in Figure 1). You could consider running the Android Studio as an Administrator. So, right-click on Android Studio from Program and Run as administrator.

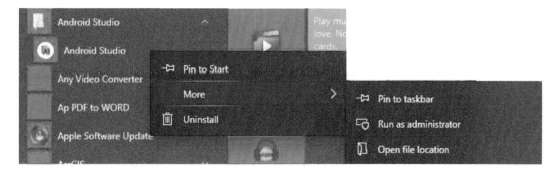

Figure 1

We now have our Android Studio launched (as in Figure 2).

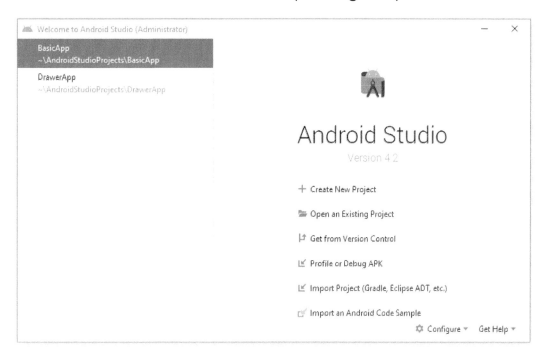

Figure 2

Next, let us create a new Android project with "Empty Activity" template. **Name**: Digital Note; **Language**: Kotlin; **API level**: 21. *Note that in creating the project for the first time, you need to connect to the internet because Android Studio might want to download some essential components into your Android Studio environment.*

So,

- Click "Create New Project"
- Select "Empty Activity" (as in Figure 3) and then Click "Next"

- Enter the Name for the app (e.g. Digital Note) and Package name (e.g. com.ajirelab.digitalnote. *Note that you could replace "ajirelab" with your desired name. However, for this book, you can retain "ajirelab". It will be part of the name of the directory for our project files*). For Language, select "Kotlin" and for Minimum SDK, select "API 21: Android 5.0 (Lollipop)". Then, click Finish (as in Figure 4)

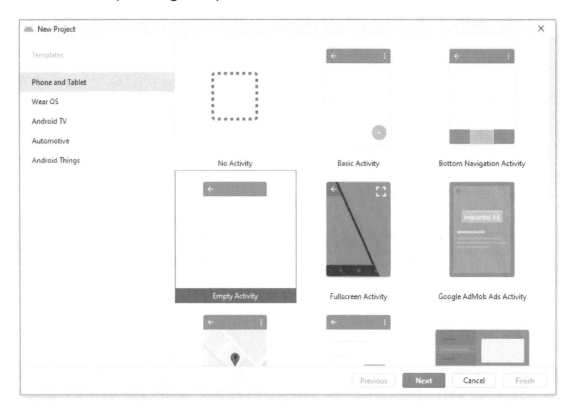

Figure 3

Figure 4

A new project named Digital Note is now created for us (as in Figure 5).

Figure 5

We can see that MainActivity.kt and activity_main.xml have been added in our new project.

Let us now proceed with the setup of the environment.

First, we need to add some essential dependencies or components that are required for our app to function as we have planned it.

- Let's open build.gradle (Project: Digital_Note) and comment out the line for jcenter by preceding it with // (as in Figure 6). By commenting it, the compiler will just ignore it and not read it as a code block. We have to comment it because it will soon be shut down and also, we already have mavenCentral() which can serve the same purpose that it's supposed to serve.

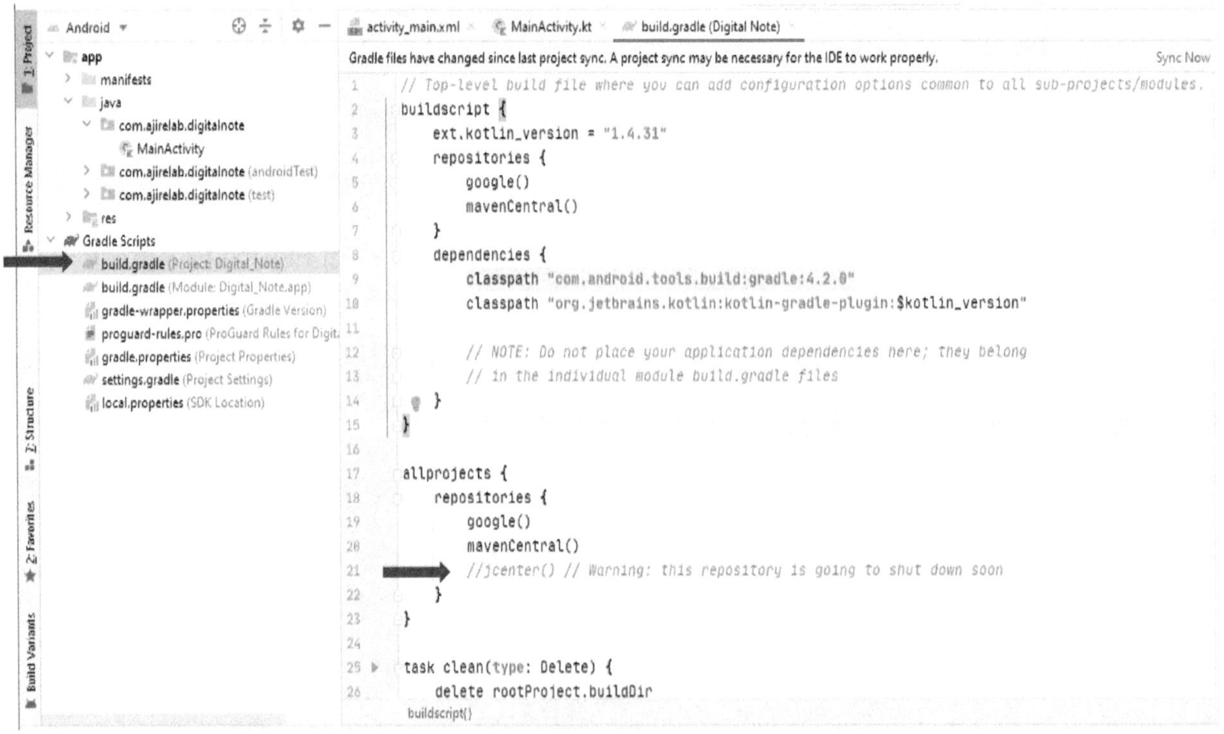

Figure 6

- Next, let us double-click gradle.properties (Project Properties) (as in Figure 7) and add the following line of code to enable Jetifier:

```
android.enableJetifier=true
```

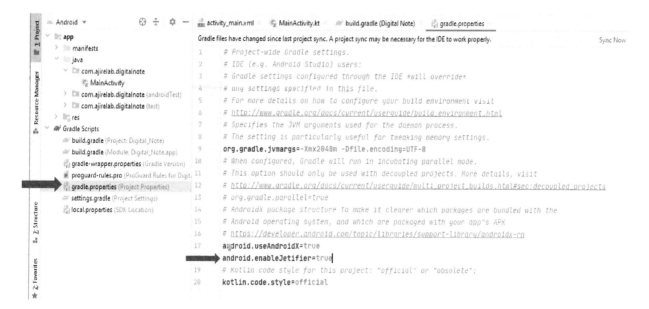

Figure 7

- Next, let us double-click **build.gradle (Module: Digital_Note.app)** to open it. Then, we will make the following additions (as in Figure 8):
  - Add `id 'kotlin-kapt'` to the block for Plugins
  - Add the following to android block

```
buildFeatures {
    viewBinding = true
}
```

  This enables view binding for our project.
  - Add the following dependencies to the dependencies block.

```
//Lifecycle dependencies
def lifecycle_version = "2.4.0"

implementation "androidx.lifecycle:lifecycle-viewmodel-
ktx:$lifecycle_version"

implementation "androidx.lifecycle:lifecycle-livedata-
ktx:$lifecycle_version"

implementation "androidx.lifecycle:lifecycle-common-
java8:$lifecycle_version"


//Room dependencies
def roomVersion = "2.3.0"
```

10

```
implementation "androidx.room:room-runtime:$roomVersion"

kapt "androidx.room:room-compiler:$roomVersion"

androidTestImplementation "androidx.room:room-
testing:$roomVersion"
```

// Preference library - Kotlin
```
implementation 'androidx.preference:preference-ktx:1.1.1'
```

//For Kotlin Coroutine
```
implementation "androidx.room:room-ktx:$roomVersion"

implementation 'org.jetbrains.kotlinx:kotlinx-coroutines-
core:1.5.0'

implementation 'org.jetbrains.kotlinx:kotlinx-coroutines-
android:1.5.0'
```

```
26          compileOptions {
27              sourceCompatibility JavaVersion.VERSION_1_8
28              targetCompatibility JavaVersion.VERSION_1_8
29          }
30          kotlinOptions {
31              jvmTarget = '1.0'
32          }
33  ──►     buildFeatures {
34              viewBinding = true
35          }
36
37      }
38
39      dependencies {
40
41          implementation "org.jetbrains.kotlin:kotlin-stdlib:$kotlin_version"
42          implementation 'androidx.core:core-ktx:1.7.0'
43          implementation 'androidx.appcompat:appcompat:1.4.1'
44          implementation 'com.google.android.material:material:1.5.0'
45          implementation 'androidx.constraintlayout:constraintlayout:2.1.3'
46          testImplementation 'junit:junit:4.+'
47          androidTestImplementation 'androidx.test.ext:junit:1.1.3'
48          androidTestImplementation 'androidx.test.espresso:espresso-core:3.4.0'
49
50  ──►     // Lifecycle dependencies
51          def lifecycle_version = "2.4.0"
52          implementation "androidx.lifecycle:lifecycle-viewmodel-ktx:$lifecycle_version"
53          implementation "androidx.lifecycle:lifecycle-livedata-ktx:$lifecycle_version"
54          implementation "androidx.lifecycle:lifecycle-common-java8:$lifecycle_version"
55
56          // Room dependencies
57          def roomVersion = "2.3.0"
58          implementation "androidx.room:room-runtime:$roomVersion"
59          kapt "androidx.room:room-compiler:$roomVersion"
60          androidTestImplementation "androidx.room:room-testing:$roomVersion"
61
62          // For Preference library - Kotlin
63          implementation 'androidx.preference:preference-ktx:1.1.1'
64
65          //For Kotlin Coroutine
66          implementation "androidx.room:room-ktx:$roomVersion"
67          implementation 'org.jetbrains.kotlinx:kotlinx-coroutines-core:1.5.0'
68          implementation 'org.jetbrains.kotlinx:kotlinx-coroutines-android:1.5.0'
69
70      }
```

Figure 8

In our module-level build.gradle file, we now have:

```
plugins {
    id 'com.android.application'
    id 'kotlin-android'
    id 'kotlin-kapt'
}

android {
    compileSdkVersion 31

    defaultConfig {
        applicationId "com.ajirelab.digitalnote"
        minSdkVersion 21
        targetSdkVersion 31
```

```
            versionCode 1
            versionName "1.0"
            testInstrumentationRunner "androidx.test.runner.AndroidJUnitRunner"
        }

        buildTypes {
            release {
                minifyEnabled false
                proguardFiles getDefaultProguardFile('proguard-android-
optimize.txt'), 'proguard-rules.pro'
            }
        }
        compileOptions {
            sourceCompatibility JavaVersion.VERSION_1_8
            targetCompatibility JavaVersion.VERSION_1_8
        }
        kotlinOptions {
            jvmTarget = '1.8'
        }
        buildFeatures {
            viewBinding = true
        }
    }

    dependencies {

        implementation "org.jetbrains.kotlin:kotlin-stdlib:$kotlin_version"
        implementation 'androidx.core:core-ktx:1.7.0'
        implementation 'androidx.appcompat:appcompat:1.4.1'
        implementation 'com.google.android.material:material:1.5.0'
        implementation 'androidx.constraintlayout:constraintlayout:2.1.3'
        testImplementation 'junit:junit:4.+'
        androidTestImplementation 'androidx.test.ext:junit:1.1.3'
        androidTestImplementation 'androidx.test.espresso:espresso-core:3.4.0'

        // Lifecycle dependencies
        def lifecycle_version = "2.4.0"
        implementation "androidx.lifecycle:lifecycle-viewmodel-
ktx:$lifecycle_version"
        implementation "androidx.lifecycle:lifecycle-livedata-
ktx:$lifecycle_version"
        implementation "androidx.lifecycle:lifecycle-common-
java8:$lifecycle_version"

        // Room dependencies
        def roomVersion = "2.3.0"
        implementation "androidx.room:room-runtime:$roomVersion"
        kapt "androidx.room:room-compiler:$roomVersion"
        androidTestImplementation "androidx.room:room-testing:$roomVersion"

        // For Preference library - Kotlin
        implementation 'androidx.preference:preference-ktx:1.1.1'

        //For Kotlin Coroutine
        implementation "androidx.room:room-ktx:$roomVersion"
        implementation 'org.jetbrains.kotlinx:kotlinx-coroutines-core:1.5.0'
        implementation 'org.jetbrains.kotlinx:kotlinx-coroutines-android:1.5.0'

    }
```

➕ Next, with our internet on, let us sync the project by clicking 'Sync Now' (as In Figure 9).

Figure 9

After successful synchronization, we are good to go with the app development. In the next stage, we will enable version control for our project. Note that internet is not required at subsequent stages for now.

STAGE 3
Enabling Version Control for this Project in Android Studio Using Git

Git is a free and open-source version control software that we can use to easily keep track of the changes we make to our software projects without the need of creating duplicates. With Git, we can roll back to previous version of our codes, and we can also connect to a remote repository.

If we do not have Git already installed on our computer system, we will need to download it from the official website using any of the following links- depending on our Operating System.

Windows: https://git-scm.com/download/win

Linux and Unix: https://git-scm.com/download/linux

macOS: https://git-scm.com/download/mac

Example of the download page for Windows OS is shown in Figure 10.

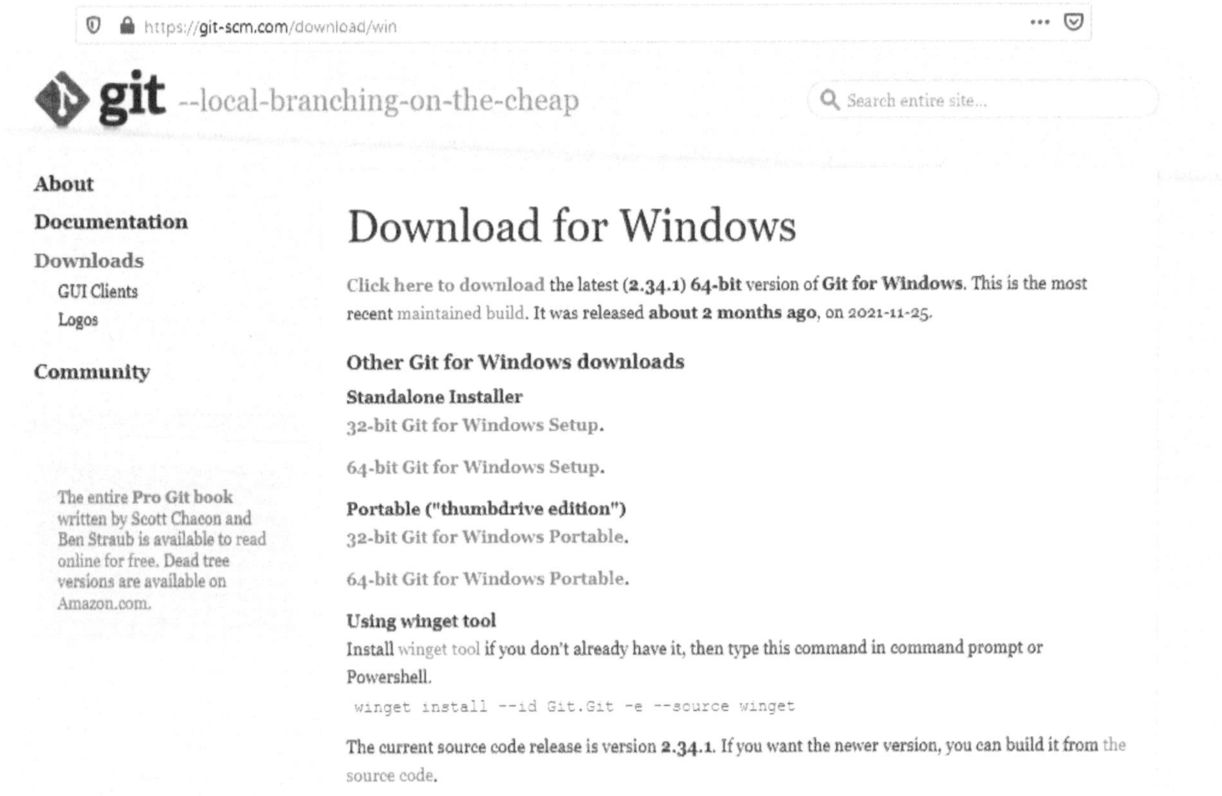

Figure 10

So, let us download and install the Git software.

After successful installation, we can return to Android Studio.

With the implementation of version control, we will be able to track changes that we are making to our project's codes and files.

Now in Android Studio, let us first check to see if Android Studio auto-detect Git (as in Figure 11).

To check, go to File menu >> Settings >> Version Control >> Git >> In the "Path to Git executable", we should see: Auto-detected: C:\\Program Files\Git\cmd\git.exe. >> Then, click "Test" to see the version of the Git installed. >> click OK.

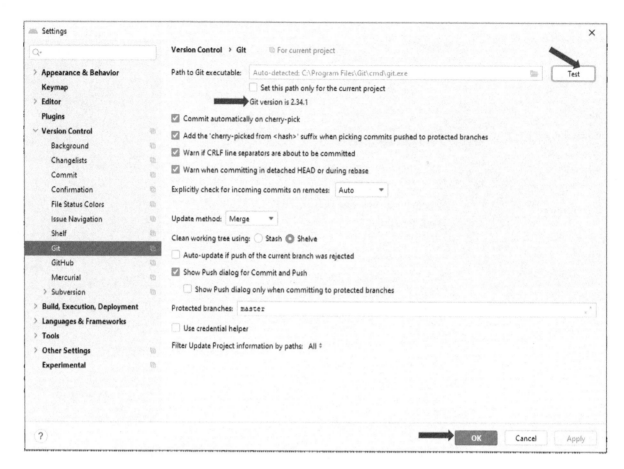

Figure 11

Next, click VCS from Menu bar >> click Enable Version Control Integration (as in Figure 12) >> select Git (if it's not already selected) >> OK (as in Figure 13).

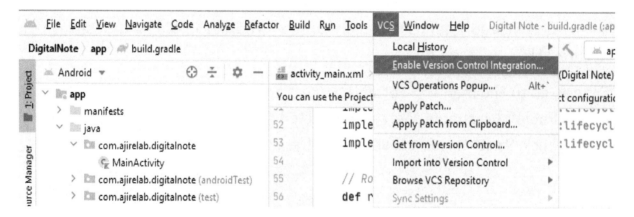

Figure 12

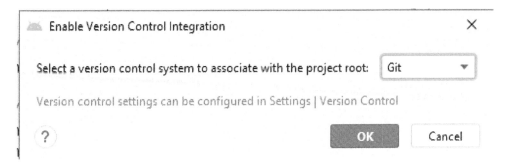

Figure 13

Now, a new tab named 'Commit' should have been added under 'Project' at the left side of the Android Studio window (as in Figure 14). Also, all the file names in the project should turn red in colour; this is because we have not staged or added them for commit yet.

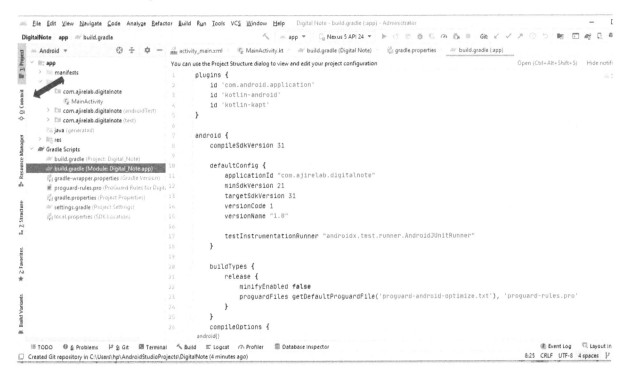

Figure 14

Next, let's click the Commit tab below the Project tab on the left side of the window. Then, mark the "Unversioned Files" (as in Figure 15). Then, enter a commit message i.e. the description of the commit (e.g. Commit done at Stage 3) (above the commit button). Then, click "Commit".

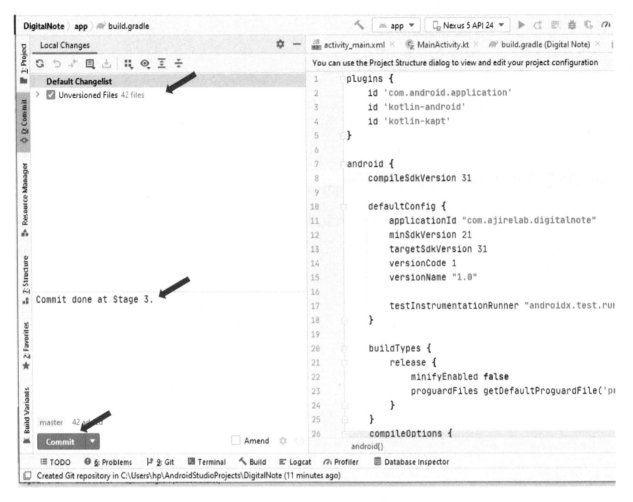

Figure 15

In the dialog box for code analysis, showing information about the number of errors and warnings (as in Figure 16), ignore it and just click "Commit".

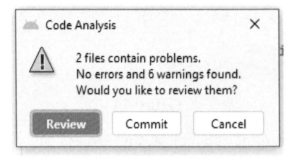

Figure 16

We now have all the files committed. By now, the names of our files should have been changed back to black. Let us now click the 'Project' tab above the 'Commit' tab.

STAGE 4

Addition of App Logo and the Needed Icons to the Drawable Directory

The name of our app logo is new_logo.PNG (as shown in Figure 17).

Figure 17

Note that the app logo icon should be 512px by 512px. I designed the app logo using CorelDraw software.

We will copy the logo from its location on the system (by right-clicking on it and then clicking 'copy'), then, we will move to Android Studio, right-click on "drawable" directory under "res" and then click "paste" (as in Figure 18).

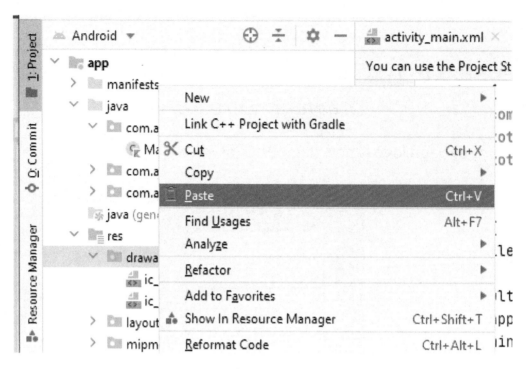

Figure 18

In the dialog box shown for destination directory, choose drawable (as in Figure 19), and click OK.

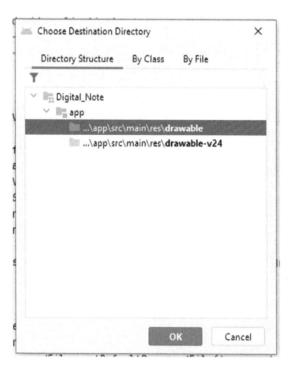

Figure 19

In the "Copy" dialog box (as in Figure 20) shown next, we can just retain the name and click OK.

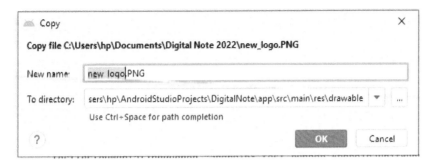

Figure 20

**We are to follow the same procedure to add another image named: my_app_icon.PNG

In the dialog box for 'Add File to Git' (as in Figure 21), mark "Remember, don't ask again" and then click 'Cancel'. We will add it later during commit.

Figure 21

Our app logo should have now been added to our drawable directory.

Next, we will add all the icons to be used for each Bottom Navigation menu item (and in other screens or aspects of the app) to the drawable directory (From 'res' >> right-click on 'drawable' >> click 'New' >> click 'Vector Assets' >> Choose a clipart and give it a name and change its color if necessary >> Next >> Finish).

The following icons should be added: ic_assignment, ic_home, ic_settings, ic_delete, ic_search (white version and black version), and ic_add (white).

For example, to add Home icon, from res >> right-click on drawable >> click 'New' >> click 'Vector Assets' (as in Figure 22) >> Choose a clipart (as in Figure 23) and give it a name (as in Figure 24) and change its color if necessary (for the Home icon, we are retaining the black color) >> click 'Next' >> click 'Finish' (as in Figure 25).

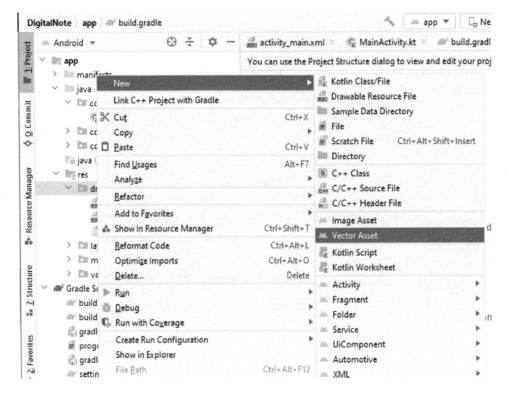

Figure 22

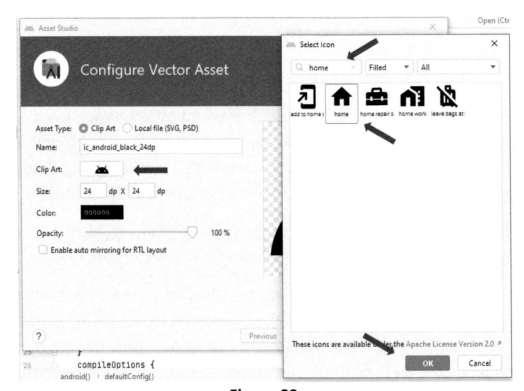

Figure 23

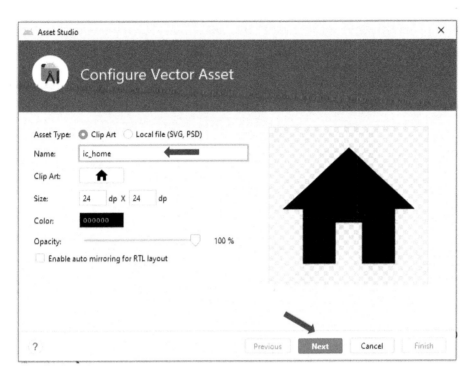

Figure 24

Figure 25

To add the other icons to the drawable directory, we are to follow the same procedure we used for adding home icon.

After adding all the needed icons, your drawable directory should have contents as shown in Figure 26.

Figure 26

STAGE 5
Modification of colors.xml and themes.xml

At this stage, we will be modifying the existing colors and themes to suit our desire.

Modification of colors

First, we will open colors.xml (res >> values >> colors.xml) and add our custom colors as follows.

```xml
<!--    These are my custom colors-->
<color name="my_primary_color">#F59707</color>
<color name="my_primary_dark_color">#B75825</color>
<color name="my_accent_color">#D81B60</color>
<color name="my_light_green_color">#76BF5E</color>
<color name="my_normal_green_color">#3F9224</color>
<color name="my_gold_color">#B76E25</color>
<color name="my_crimson_color">#DC143C</color>
<color name="my_white">#FFFFFF</color>
```

So, in colors.xml, we now have the content as shown in Figure 27.

```xml
activity_main.xml    MainActivity.kt    colors.xml
1    <?xml version="1.0" encoding="utf-8"?>
2    <resources>
3        <color name="purple_200">#FFBB86FC</color>
4        <color name="purple_500">#FF6200EE</color>
5        <color name="purple_700">#FF3700B3</color>
6        <color name="teal_200">#FF03DAC5</color>
7        <color name="teal_700">#FF018786</color>
8        <color name="black">#FF000000</color>
9        <color name="white">#FFFFFFFF</color>
10
11       <!--    These are my custom colors -->
12       <color name="my_primary_color">#F59707</color>
13       <color name="my_primary_dark_color">#B75825</color>
14       <color name="my_accent_color">#D81B60</color>
15       <color name="my_light_green_color">#76BF5E</color>
16       <color name="my_normal_green_color">#3F9224</color>
17       <color name="my_gold_color">#B76E25</color>
18       <color name="my_crimson_color">#DC143C</color>
19       <color name="my_white">#FFFFFF</color>
20
21    </resources>
```

Figure 27

26

Next, we will go to themes.xml (res >> values >> themes >> themes.xml) and change the references accordingly as follows:

```
<!-- Primary brand color. -->
<item name="colorPrimary">@color/my_primary_color</item>
<item
name="colorPrimaryVariant">@color/my_primary_dark_color</item>
<item name="colorOnPrimary">@color/white</item>
<!-- Secondary brand color. -->
<item name="colorSecondary">@color/my_accent_color</item>
<item name="colorSecondaryVariant">@color/teal_700</item>
<item name="colorOnSecondary">@color/black</item>
```

Also, we will change the references in theme(night) (res >> values >> themes >> themes.xml (night)) as follows:

```
<!-- Primary brand color. -->
<item name="colorPrimary">@color/purple_200</item>
<item
name="colorPrimaryVariant">@color/my_primary_dark_color</item>
<item name="colorOnPrimary">@color/black</item>
<!-- Secondary brand color. -->
<item name="colorSecondary">@color/my_accent_color</item>
<item name="colorSecondaryVariant">@color/my_accent_color</item>
<item name="colorOnSecondary">@color/black</item>
```

Modification of theme style to NoActionBar.

Inside the theme.xml and theme.xml(night), we will change DarkActionBar to NoActionBar in the style tag. i.e.

```
<style name="Theme.DigitalNote"
parent="Theme.MaterialComponents.DayNight.NoActionBar">
```

So, in themes.xml, we now have content as shown in Figure 28.

```
   activity_main.xml      MainActivity.kt      themes.xml ⊗
1      <resources xmlns:tools="http://schemas.
2          <!-- Base application theme. -->              Close. Alt-Click to Close Others
3          <style name="Theme.DigitalNote" parent="Theme.MaterialComponents.DayNight.NoActionBar">
4              <!-- Primary brand color. -->
5              <item name="colorPrimary">@color/my_primary_color</item>
6              <item name="colorPrimaryVariant">@color/my_primary_dark_color</item>
7              <item name="colorOnPrimary">@color/white</item>
8              <!-- Secondary brand color. -->
9              <item name="colorSecondary">@color/my_accent_color</item>
10             <item name="colorSecondaryVariant">@color/teal_700</item>
11             <item name="colorOnSecondary">@color/black</item>
12
13             <!-- Status bar color. -->
14             <item name="android:statusBarColor" tools:targetApi="l">?attr/colorPrimaryVariant</item>
15             <!-- Customize your theme here. -->
16         </style>
17     </resources>
```

Figure 28

Also, in night\themes.xml, we now have content as shown in Figure 29

```
   activity_main.xml      MainActivity.kt      night\themes.xml
1      <resources xmlns:tools="http://schemas.android.com/tools">
2          <!-- Base application theme. -->
3          <style name="Theme.DigitalNote" parent="Theme.MaterialComponents.DayNight.NoActionBar">
4              <!-- Primary brand color. -->
5              <item name="colorPrimary">@color/purple_200</item>
6              <item name="colorPrimaryVariant">@color/my_primary_dark_color</item>
7              <item name="colorOnPrimary">@color/black</item>
8              <!-- Secondary brand color. -->
9              <item name="colorSecondary">@color/my_accent_color</item>
10             <item name="colorSecondaryVariant">@color/my_accent_color</item>
11             <item name="colorOnSecondary">@color/black</item>
12
13             <!-- Status bar color. -->
14             <item name="android:statusBarColor" tools:targetApi="l">?attr/colorPrimaryVariant</item>
15             <!-- Customize your theme here. -->
16         </style>
17     </resources>
```

Figure 29

STAGE 6
Update of strings.xml Resource File
(plus commit changes)

At this stage, we will be adding some string resources to our strings.xml file. The string resources are the key words (such as name for menu, text for text fields or views, text for buttons, among others) that we have planned to include in our app.

So, for now, the content of our strings.xml should be updated to:

```xml
<resources>
    <string name="app_name">Digital Note</string>

    <string name="action_settings">Settings</string>
    <string name="action_new_note">New Note</string>

    <string name="menu_home">Home</string>
    <string name="menu_settings">Settings</string>
    <string name="menu_search">Search</string>

    <string name="note_category">Note Category</string>
    <string name="note_title">Note Title</string>
    <string name="note_details">Note Details</string>

    <string name="cancel">Cancel</string>
    <string name="save">Save</string>

    <string name="note_saved">Note Saved Successfully.</string>
    <string name="note_updated">Note Updated.</string>
    <string name="note_deleted">Note Deleted.</string>
    <string name="not_saved">Not Saved.</string>

    <string name="open_note">Open Note</string>
    <string name="app_image_description">App logo description</string>
    <string name="enter_your_password">Enter your password</string>
</resources>
```

Commit changes

After updating the strings.xml file, let us now commit our changes from stage 4 to this stage 6.

Click the Commit tab below the Project tab on the left side of the window (as in Figure 30). Then, mark the "Default Changelist" and "Unversioned Files". Then, enter a commit message i.e. the description of the commit (e.g. Commit done at Stage 6.) (above the commit button) > click "Commit".

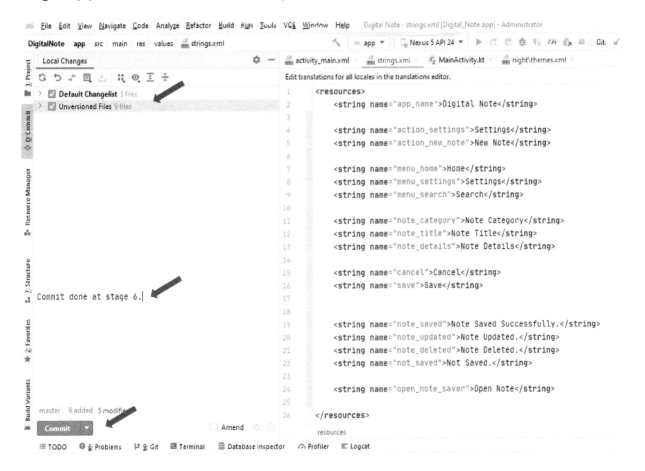

Figure 30

In the dialog box for code analysis, showing info about the number of errors and warnings (as in Figure 31), ignore it and just click "Commit".

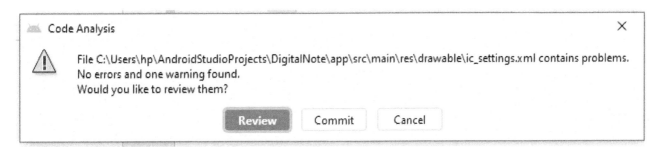

Figure 31

We now have all the files committed. Let us now click the 'Project' tab above the 'Commit' tab.

STAGE 7
Addition of a New Activity (named EntryActivity) from Empty Activity Template

The EntryActivity will later be the launcher activity. It will be the first screen that users will see when they launch our app.

The activity is for users to sign-in if they enabled Security from Settings screen, and gain full access to the app.

NB: At first launch, the user will gain full access to the app without any sign-in.

To create the activity, let's go to File menu >> New >> Activity >> Empty Activity >> then click 'Next' >> Activity Name: EntryActivity; Ensure that the language is Kotlin, and 'Generate a Layout File' is marked >> Finish (as in Figure 32).

Figure 32

Now, we have EntryActivity.kt and activity_entry.xml.

Let us first open activity_entry.xml and design the user interface for the EntryActivity.

So, for the activity_entry.xml, we will add an image view (id= imageWelcome), an EditText view for Password entry (id = edtPassword and with visibility of "gone") and a button (id= btnEntry). The EditText view for entering password will be invisible at first launch, it will only be made visible if the user should enable Security under Settings screen.

So, let us update the code for activity_entry.xml to the following:

```xml
<?xml version="1.0" encoding="utf-8"?>
<androidx.constraintlayout.widget.ConstraintLayout
xmlns:android="http://schemas.android.com/apk/res/android"
    xmlns:app="http://schemas.android.com/apk/res-auto"
    xmlns:tools="http://schemas.android.com/tools"
    android:layout_width="match_parent"
    android:layout_height="match_parent"
    tools:context=".EntryActivity">

    <ImageView
        android:id="@+id/imageWelcome"
        android:layout_width="200dp"
        android:layout_height="200dp"
        android:layout_marginTop="50dp"
        android:contentDescription="@string/app_image_description"
        app:layout_constraintEnd_toEndOf="parent"
        app:layout_constraintStart_toStartOf="parent"
        app:layout_constraintTop_toTopOf="parent"
        app:srcCompat="@drawable/new_logo" />

    <EditText
        android:id="@+id/edtPassword"
        android:layout_width="0dp"
        android:layout_height="wrap_content"
        android:layout_marginStart="24dp"
        android:layout_marginTop="24dp"
        android:layout_marginEnd="24dp"
        android:ems="10"
        android:hint="@string/enter_your_password"
        android:inputType="textPassword"
        android:visibility="gone"
        app:layout_constraintEnd_toEndOf="parent"
        app:layout_constraintStart_toStartOf="parent"
        app:layout_constraintTop_toBottomOf="@+id/imageWelcome" />

    <Button
        android:id="@+id/btnEntry"
        android:layout_width="wrap_content"
        android:layout_height="wrap_content"
```

```
android:layout_marginTop="16dp"
android:backgroundTint="@color/my_primary_color"
android:text="@string/open_note"
android:textSize="20sp"
app:layout_constraintEnd_toEndOf="parent"
app:layout_constraintStart_toStartOf="parent"
app:layout_constraintTop_toBottomOf="@+id/edtPassword" />
```

```
</androidx.constraintlayout.widget.ConstraintLayout>
```

From the Design view, we have the following layout as shown in Figure 33.

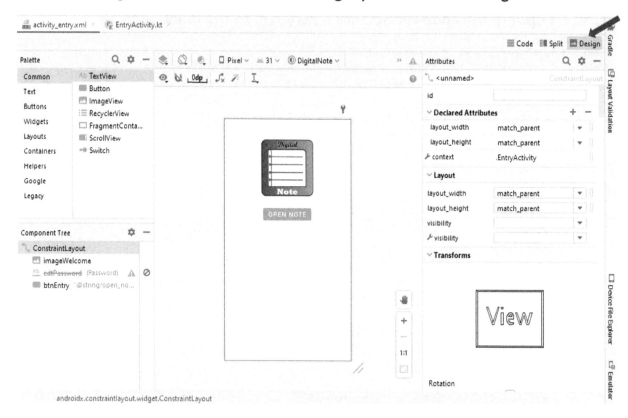

Figure 33

Notice that to the right of the "Design" tab, we have "Split" and then "Code". When the Split tab is clicked, both Design and Code view will be shown.

Next, in the EntryActivity.kt, we will activate view binding and utilize it accordingly.

View binding is a feature that allows us to write codes that interact with views easily. It is a replacement for findViewById. It generates a binding class for each XML layout file present in the Android project.

In addition, an instance of the binding class contains direct references to all views that have been assigned an id in the corresponding layout.

Note that we have already enabled view binding in project level build.gradle file at Stage 2 with the following lines of code:

```
buildFeatures {
    viewBinding = true
}
```

Now that it is enabled, to use it in our Activity (for example, EntryActivity.kt), we will first create an instance of the binding class. For example:

```
private lateinit var binding: ActivityEntryBinding
```

NB: The ActivityEntryBinding type will be generated by default and it is associated with activity_entry.xml. In the case of activity_main.xml, we will have ActivityMainBinding generated.

Second, we will call the static inflate( ) method included in the generated binding class and assign it to the binding variable earlier declared. For example:

```
binding                                    =
ActivityEntryBinding.inflate(layoutInflater)
```

Third, we will get a reference to the root view (by calling the Kotlin 'root' property syntax) and assign it to an immutable variable named 'view'. For example:

```
val view = binding.root
```

Fourth, we will pass the root view to setContentView( ) to make it the active view on the screen. For example:

```
setContentView(view)
```

That's it.

We can now use an instance of the binding class to make reference to any of the views in the layout file. For example:

```
binding.btnEntry      (This makes reference to the view with the id-
btnEntry)
```

Implementation of security password for sign-in will be done later.

So, let us update EntryActivity.kt as follows:

```kotlin
package com.ajirelab.digitalnote

import android.content.Intent
import androidx.appcompat.app.AppCompatActivity
import android.os.Bundle
import com.ajirelab.digitalnote.databinding.ActivityEntryBinding

class EntryActivity : AppCompatActivity() {
    private lateinit var binding: ActivityEntryBinding    // for view
binding (a)

    override fun onCreate(savedInstanceState: Bundle?) {
        super.onCreate(savedInstanceState)
        binding = ActivityEntryBinding.inflate(layoutInflater) // for
view binding (b)
        val view = binding.root               // for view binding (c)
        setContentView(view)                  // for view binding (d)

        /*With these, when the users click the button_entry, they will
be redirected to MainActivity screen*/
//The code for activating Password entry will be added later.

        binding.btnEntry.setOnClickListener {
            val intent = Intent (this, MainActivity::class.java)
            startActivity(intent)
        }

    }
}
```

Next, we will make the EntryActivity to be the launcher activity for the app (by adding intent-filter tag). So, let us go to app >> Manifest >> AndroidManifest.xml (as in Figure 34).

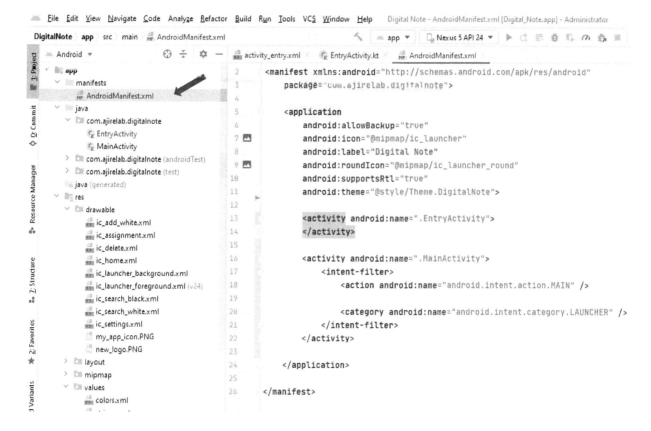

Figure 34

Now, we will remove **intent-filter** from the tag for MainActivity and add it to the tag for EntryActivity.

And also, we will include **android:exported="true"** because Android 12 is our highest targeted SDK.

With the addition of **intent-filter tag** and **android:exported attribute**, the content of AndroidManifest.xml is now:

```xml
<?xml version="1.0" encoding="utf-8"?>
<manifest xmlns:android="http://schemas.android.com/apk/res/android"
    package="com.ajirelab.digitalnote">

    <application
        android:allowBackup="true"
        android:icon="@mipmap/ic_launcher"
        android:label="@string/app_name"
        android:roundIcon="@mipmap/ic_launcher_round"
        android:supportsRtl="true"
        android:theme="@style/Theme.DigitalNote">

        <activity android:name=".EntryActivity"
            android:exported="true">
```

```xml
        <intent-filter>
            <action android:name="android.intent.action.MAIN" />
            <category android:name="android.intent.category.LAUNCHER"
/>
        </intent-filter>
    </activity>

    <activity android:name=".MainActivity"/>

    </application>

</manifest>
```

STAGE 8
Addition of ActionBar Menu Items and Bottom Navigation Menu Items (plus commit changes)

First, we will create a new menu file in a new menu directory. To do this, right-click on "res" >> click New >> select "Android Resource File" >> File name= "menu" >> from Resource Type, choose "Menu" >> Note that Root element, Source set and Directory name will be added by default. >> OK. (as in Figure 35).

Figure 35

The menu created will be for the option menu items that will be on the Action Bar of MainActivity.

Now that we have menu.xml file, let's add the following code for "New Note" and "Settings" menu items.

```xml
<?xml version="1.0" encoding="utf-8"?>
<menu
xmlns:android="http://schemas.android.com/apk/res/android"
    xmlns:app="http://schemas.android.com/apk/res-auto">
    <item
        android:id="@+id/action_new_note"
        android:orderInCategory="99"
```

```
        android:title="@string/action_new_note"
        app:showAsAction="never" />

    <item
        android:id="@+id/action_settings"
        android:orderInCategory="100"
        android:title="@string/action_settings"
        app:showAsAction="never" />
</menu>
```

From the Design view, we have the following (Figure 36)

Figure 36

Addition of menu items for bottom navigation

Next, we will create a menu resource file named "bottom_navigation_menu". To do this, we will go to res >> right-click "menu" >> click 'New' >> then click 'Menu Resource File' >> we will name it 'bottom_navigation_menu' >> then click OK.

Next, we will open bottom_navigation_menu.xml and add some menu items. The menu file will be the layout for our bottom navigation bar.

The content of the bottom_navigation_menu.xml is now:

```
<?xml version="1.0" encoding="utf-8"?>
<menu xmlns:android="http://schemas.android.com/apk/res/android">
```

```
<item
    android:id="@+id/bottom_nav_home"
    android:icon="@drawable/ic_home"
    android:title="@string/menu_home" />

<item
    android:id="@+id/bottom_nav_settings"
    android:icon="@drawable/ic_settings"
    android:title="@string/menu_settings" />

<item
    android:id="@+id/bottom_nav_search"
    android:icon="@drawable/ic_search_black"
    android:title="@string/menu_search" />
</menu>
```

From the design view, we have the following (as in Figure 37)

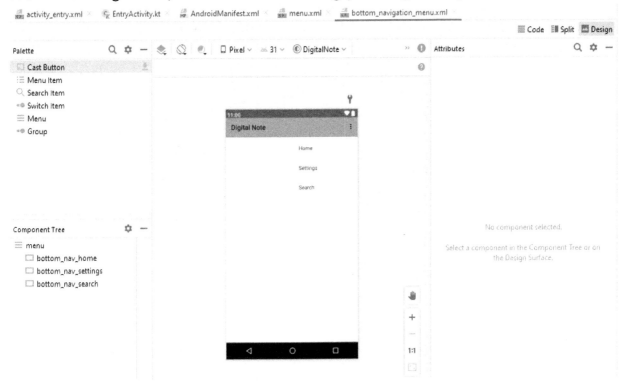

Figure 37

Next, let us commit the changes we have made at Stage 7 and stage 8.

Commit changes

Click the Commit tab below the Project tab on the left side of the window (as in Figure 38). Then, mark the "Default Changelist" and "Unversioned Files". Then, enter a commit message i.e. the description of the commit (e.g. Commit done at Stage 8.) (above the commit button) >> click "Commit".

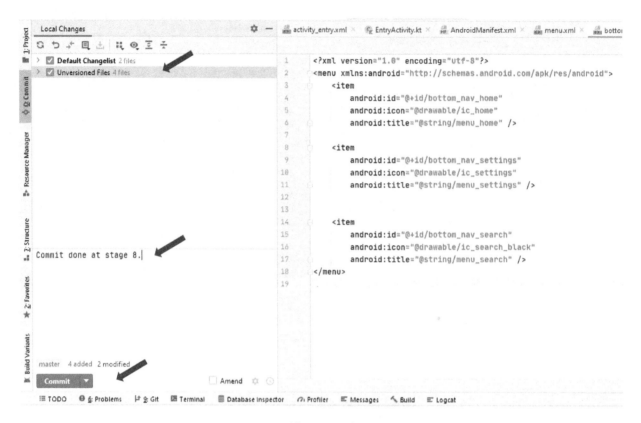

Figure 38

In the dialog box for code analysis, showing info about the number of errors and warnings (as in Figure 39), ignore it and just click "Commit".

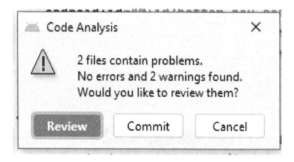

Figure 39

We now have all the files committed. Let us proceed by clicking the 'Project' tab above the 'Commit' tab.

41

STAGE 9
Addition of New Layout File (content_main.xml)

This new layout file will be the second layout file for our MainActivity. This layout file will be referenced from activity_main.xml (which is the first layout file for MainActivity). It is in this content_main.xml that we will have our RecyclerView and make reference to the xml file that will contain the CardView to be shown in the RecyclerView.

So, we will add the layout file as follows:

From res, right-click on "layout" >> New >> Layout Resource file >> File name: content_main >> then click OK (as in Figure 40).

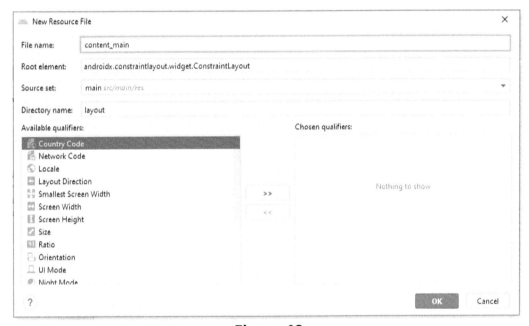

Figure 40

An empty content_main.xml is now created (as in Figure 41).

```
content_main.xml

                                                                          Code  Split  Design
1    <?xml version="1.0" encoding="utf-8"?>
2    <androidx.constraintlayout.widget.ConstraintLayout xmlns:android="http://schemas.android.com/apk/res/android"
3        android:layout_width="match_parent"
4        android:layout_height="match_parent">
5
6    </androidx.constraintlayout.widget.ConstraintLayout>
```

Figure 41

The content_main.xml is to be included and referenced in the activity_main.xml.

Next, we will update the codes in the opening tag for constraintLayout as follows:

```
<androidx.constraintlayout.widget.ConstraintLayout
xmlns:android="http://schemas.android.com/apk/res/android"
    xmlns:app="http://schemas.android.com/apk/res-auto"
    xmlns:tools="http://schemas.android.com/tools"
    android:layout_width="match_parent"
    android:layout_height="match_parent"
    app:layout_behavior="@string/appbar_scrolling_view_behavior"
    tools:context=".MainActivity"
    tools:showIn="@layout/activity_main">

</androidx.constraintlayout.widget.ConstraintLayout>
```

STAGE 10
Working on activity_main.xml

Our activity_main is going to contain a Floating Action Button to add new note, a RecyclerView for displaying the notes and there should be an AppBarLayout.
The AppBarLayout is to contain the toolbar element.

We will add a coordinator layout inside which the AppBarLayout, the <include> element for the content_main.xml (which will contain the RecyclerView) and the Floating Action Button will be housed.
Also, we will reference the bottom_navigation_menu in the BottomNavigationView in this activity_main.xml.

First, we will delete the default Hello World TextView by deleting the following highlighted code (as in Figure 42).

Figure 42

Next, let us open the app gradle file and change the version of material from 1.5.0 to 1.4.0 (as in Figure 43), and then Sync project.

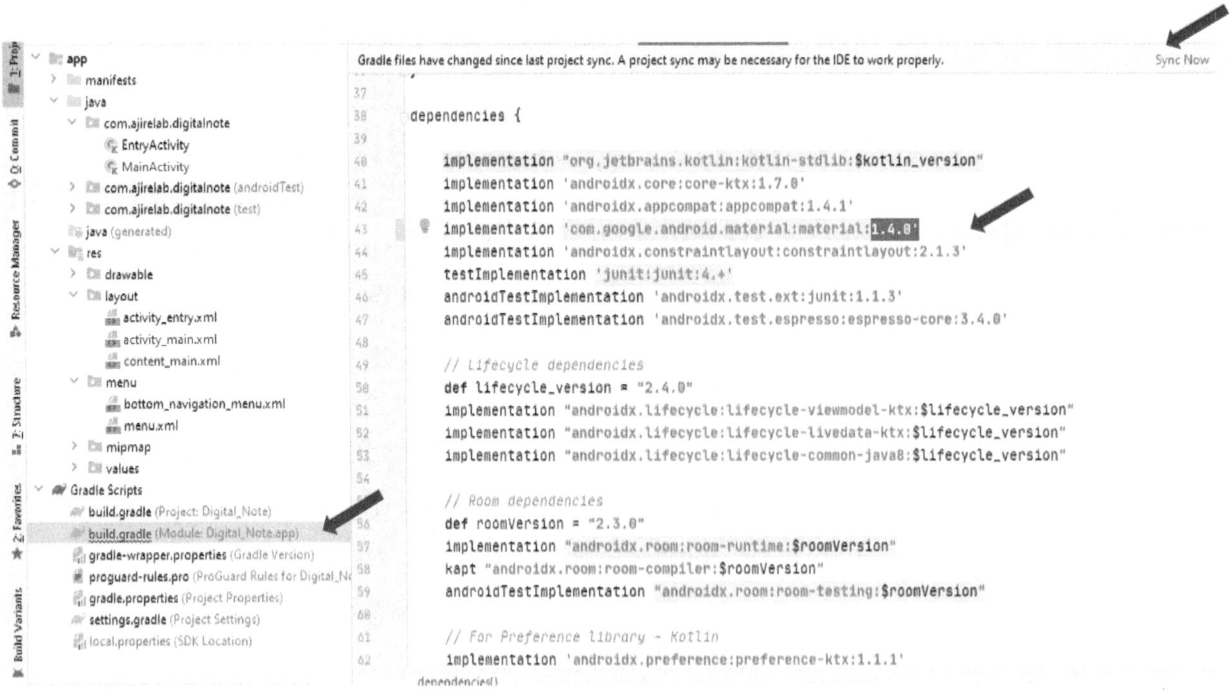

Figure 43

After successful synchronization, let us go back to our activity_main.xml.

Next, still in the Code view, let us add a BottomNavigationView. It is in it that we will reference the bottom_navigation_menu.

So, we will add the view and assign an id of bottom_nav_view to it as follows:

```
<com.google.android.material.bottomnavigation.BottomNavigationView
    android:id="@+id/bottom_nav_view"
    android:layout_width="match_parent"
    android:layout_height= "wrap_content"
    app:layout_constraintBottom_toBottomOf="parent"
    app:layout_constraintEnd_toEndOf="parent"
    app:layout_constraintStart_toStartOf="parent"
    app:menu="@menu/bottom_navigation_menu"  />
```

Now, above the BottomNavigationView, we will add a coordinatorLayout with an id of rvCoordinatorLayout.

For the CoordinatorLayout, let us add the following:

```
<androidx.coordinatorlayout.widget.CoordinatorLayout
    android:layout_width="match_parent"
    android:layout_height="0dp"
    android:id="@+id/rvCoordinatorLayout"
    app:layout_constraintBottom_toTopOf="@+id/bottom_nav_view"
    app:layout_constraintEnd_toEndOf="parent"
    app:layout_constraintStart_toStartOf="parent"
    app:layout_constraintTop_toTopOf="parent"
```

45

```
        android:background="#FFFFFF"
        android:fitsSystemWindows="true">
    </androidx.coordinatorlayout.widget.CoordinatorLayout>
```

Now, inside the CoordinatorLayout, we will add the AppBarLayout, the <include> element for the content_main.xml (which will contain the RecyclerView) and the Floating Action Button.

For the AppBarLayout, we will add the following:

```
<com.google.android.material.appbar.AppBarLayout
        style="@style/Widget.MaterialComponents.AppBarLayout.PrimarySurface"
        android:layout_width="match_parent"
        android:layout_height="wrap_content"
        android:fitsSystemWindows="true">

    <com.google.android.material.appbar.MaterialToolbar
        android:id="@+id/toolbar"
        style="@style/Widget.MaterialComponents.Toolbar.PrimarySurface"
        android:layout_width="match_parent"
        android:layout_height="?attr/actionBarSize"
        android:elevation="4dp"
        app:layout_scrollFlags="scroll|enterAlways"/>

</com.google.android.material.appbar.AppBarLayout>
```

For the <include> element, we will add the following after the AppBarLayout:

```
<include
    android:id="@+id/layout_content_main"
    layout="@layout/content_main" />
```

With the id, we can easily access and reference the views in content_main.xml using view binding from MainActivity.kt.

For the floating action button, we will add the following:

```
<com.google.android.material.floatingactionbutton.FloatingActionButton
        android:id="@+id/fab"
        android:layout_width="wrap_content"
        android:layout_height="wrap_content"
        android:layout_gravity="bottom|end"
        android:layout_margin="16dp"
        app:tint="@color/white"
        app:srcCompat="@drawable/ic_add_white" />
```

We now have the following code in activity_main.xml

```
<?xml version="1.0" encoding="utf-8"?>
<androidx.constraintlayout.widget.ConstraintLayout
    xmlns:android="http://schemas.android.com/apk/res/android"
    xmlns:app="http://schemas.android.com/apk/res-auto"
    xmlns:tools="http://schemas.android.com/tools"
    android:layout_width="match_parent"
```

```
        android:layout_height="match_parent"
        tools:context=".MainActivity">
        <!--I added a coordinator layout inside which the AppBarLayout,
        the <include> element for the content_main.xml (which will contain the
recycler view) and the Floating Action Button were housed.-->

        <!-- I assigned an Id (rvCoordinatorLayout) and a background color to the
coordinatorlayout. These will be useful when it is time to change the
background color from Settings screen switch preference.-->

        <androidx.coordinatorlayout.widget.CoordinatorLayout
            android:layout_width="match_parent"
            android:layout_height="0dp"
            android:id="@+id/rvCoordinatorLayout"
            app:layout_constraintBottom_toTopOf="@+id/bottom_nav_view"
            app:layout_constraintEnd_toEndOf="parent"
            app:layout_constraintStart_toStartOf="parent"
            app:layout_constraintTop_toTopOf="parent"
            android:background="#FFFFFF"
            android:fitsSystemWindows="true">

            <com.google.android.material.appbar.AppBarLayout
              style="@style/Widget.MaterialComponents.AppBarLayout.PrimarySurface"
                android:layout_width="match_parent"
                android:layout_height="wrap_content"
                android:fitsSystemWindows="true">

                <com.google.android.material.appbar.MaterialToolbar
                    android:id="@+id/toolbar"
                  style="@style/Widget.MaterialComponents.Toolbar.PrimarySurface"
                    android:layout_width="match_parent"
                    android:layout_height="?attr/actionBarSize"
                    android:elevation="4dp"
                    app:layout_scrollFlags="scroll|enterAlways"/>

            </com.google.android.material.appbar.AppBarLayout>

            <include
                android:id="@+id/layout_content_main"
                layout="@layout/content_main" />

<com.google.android.material.floatingactionbutton.FloatingActionButton
                android:id="@+id/fab"
                android:layout_width="wrap_content"
                android:layout_height="wrap_content"
                android:layout_gravity="bottom|end"
                android:layout_margin="16dp"
                app:tint="@color/white"
                app:srcCompat="@drawable/ic_add_white" />
</androidx.coordinatorlayout.widget.CoordinatorLayout>
        <!--Also, I referenced the bottom_navigation_menu in the
BottomNavigationView I added.-->

        <com.google.android.material.bottomnavigation.BottomNavigationView
            android:id="@+id/bottom_nav_view"
            android:layout_width="match_parent"
            android:layout_height= "wrap_content"
            app:layout_constraintBottom_toBottomOf="parent"
            app:layout_constraintEnd_toEndOf="parent"
```

```
        app:layout_constraintStart_toStartOf="parent"
        app:menu="@menu/bottom_navigation_menu" />
</androidx.constraintlayout.widget.ConstraintLayout>
```

The current design view of activity_main.xml is show in Figure 44.

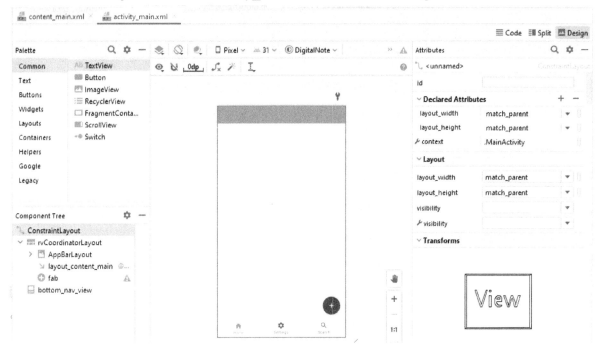

Figure 44

Next, let us choose to show system UI by clicking the 'View Options' icon and then selecting 'Show system UI' as in Figure 45.

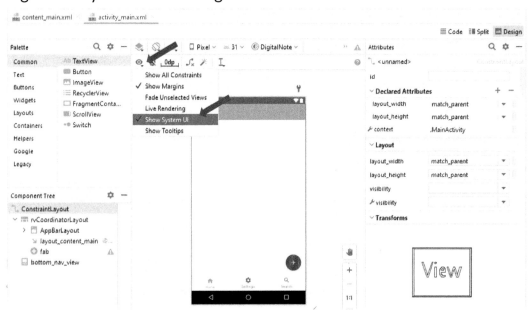

Figure 45

In the next stage, we will inflate our menus and bottom navigation in MainActivity.

STAGE 11
Inflating Menus and Implementing Bottom Navigation in MainActivity.kt
(plus commit and app testing in the emulator)

The content of MainActivity.kt before updating it is shown in Figure 46.

```
content_main.xml ×    activity_main.xml ×    MainActivity.kt ×    bottom_navigation_menu.xml ×
1        package com.ajirelab.digitalnote
2
3        import androidx.appcompat.app.AppCompatActivity
4        import android.os.Bundle
5
6        class MainActivity : AppCompatActivity() {
7            override fun onCreate(savedInstanceState: Bundle?) {
8                super.onCreate(savedInstanceState)
9                setContentView(R.layout.activity_main)
10           }
11       }
```

Figure 46

Let us now update the file.

First, we will activate view binding by adding the following codes:

```
private lateinit var binding: ActivityMainBinding    // for view binding (a)
```

>   (to be added before onCreate method)

NB: Press Alt+Enter on ActivityMainBinding to import it.

Next, inside the onCreate, we will add the other codes for view binding as follows:

```
binding = ActivityMainBinding.inflate(layoutInflater) // for view binding (b)
val view = binding.root                               // for view binding (c)
setContentView(view)                                  // for view binding (d)
```

Next, still inside onCreate method, we will initialize the toolbar, fab and bottomNavMenu using the view binding:

```
val toolbar = binding.toolbar
val fab = binding.fab
val bottomNavView = binding.bottomNavView   //for initializing and
    binding the    bottom navigation view
```

Next, we will pass the toolbar to setSupportActionBar( )

```
setSupportActionBar(toolbar)
```

Next, let us add a toast code to activate the floating action button for now:

```
fab.setOnClickListener {
    Toast.makeText(this, "New note will be added",
Toast.LENGTH_SHORT).show()
}
```

NB: Press Alt+Enter on Toast to import it.

Still inside the onCreate method, let us add Toast to each of the bottom navigation menu items for now, using setOnItemSelectedListener from the bottomNavView.

```
bottomNavView.setOnItemSelectedListener {
        when(it.itemId) {
            R.id.bottom_nav_home -> Toast.makeText(
                applicationContext,
                "Home screen clicked",
                Toast.LENGTH_SHORT
            ).show()

            R.id.bottom_nav_search -> Toast.makeText(
                applicationContext,
                "Search clicked",
                Toast.LENGTH_SHORT
            ).show()

            R.id.bottom_nav_settings -> Toast.makeText(
                applicationContext,
                "Settings clicked",
                Toast.LENGTH_SHORT
            ).show()
        }
        true
    }
```

Now, outside or below onCreate method, we will override onCreateOptionsMenu to inflate the menu item in the ActionBar of the Main Activity.

```
override fun onCreateOptionsMenu(menu: Menu): Boolean {
    // Inflate the menu; this adds items to the action bar if it is
present.
    menuInflater.inflate(R.menu.menu, menu)
    return true
}
```

NB: Press Alt+Enter on Menu underlined in red to import it.

Still for the Main Activity ActionBar option menu items, we will override onOptionsItemSelected (to be done after onCreateOptionsMenu). We will assign Toast messages to the menu items for now.

```kotlin
    override fun onOptionsItemSelected(item: MenuItem): Boolean {
            if (item.itemId == R.id.action_settings){
                Toast.makeText(
                applicationContext,
                "Action bar settings clicked",
                Toast.LENGTH_SHORT
            ).show()

            }

            if (item.itemId == R.id.action_new_note){
                Toast.makeText(
                applicationContext,
                "New note clicked",
                Toast.LENGTH_SHORT
            ).show()

            }
            return super.onOptionsItemSelected(item)
        }
```

NB: Press Alt+Enter on MenuItem underlined in red to import it

That's all we have to do to implement the bottom navigation bar and others.

Now, in our MainActivity.kt, we have the following codes for now:

```kotlin
package com.ajirelab.digitalnote

import androidx.appcompat.app.AppCompatActivity
import android.os.Bundle
import android.view.Menu
import android.view.MenuItem
import android.widget.Toast
import com.ajirelab.digitalnote.databinding.ActivityMainBinding

class MainActivity : AppCompatActivity() {
    private lateinit var binding: ActivityMainBinding // for view binding (a)

    override fun onCreate(savedInstanceState: Bundle?) {
        super.onCreate(savedInstanceState)
        binding = ActivityMainBinding.inflate(layoutInflater) // for view binding (b)
        val view = binding.root              // for view binding (c)
        setContentView(view)                 // for view binding (d)

        val toolbar = binding.toolbar     //for initializing and binding the toolbar
        val fab = binding.fab     ////for initializing and binding the floating action button
        val bottomNavView = binding.bottomNavView    //for initializing and binding the bottom navigation view

        setSupportActionBar(toolbar)
```

51

```
fab.setOnClickListener {
    Toast.makeText(this, "New note will be added",
        Toast.LENGTH_SHORT).show()
}

bottomNavView.setOnItemSelectedListener {
    when (it.itemId) {
        R.id.bottom_nav_home -> Toast.makeText(
            applicationContext,
            "Home screen clicked",
            Toast.LENGTH_SHORT
        ).show()

        R.id.bottom_nav_search -> Toast.makeText(
            applicationContext,
            "Search clicked",
            Toast.LENGTH_SHORT
        ).show()

        R.id.bottom_nav_settings -> Toast.makeText(
            applicationContext,
            "Settings clicked",
            Toast.LENGTH_SHORT
        ).show()
    }
    true
}
}

override fun onCreateOptionsMenu(menu: Menu): Boolean {
    // Inflate the menu; this adds items to the action bar if it is
present.
    menuInflater.inflate(R.menu.menu, menu)
    return true
}

override fun onOptionsItemSelected(item: MenuItem): Boolean {
    if (item.itemId == R.id.action_settings){
        Toast.makeText(
            applicationContext,
            "Action bar settings clicked",
            Toast.LENGTH_SHORT
        ).show()
    }

    if (item.itemId == R.id.action_new_note){
        Toast.makeText(
            applicationContext,
            "New note clicked",
            Toast.LENGTH_SHORT
        ).show()
    }
    return super.onOptionsItemSelected(item)
}
}
```

At this stage, let us commit our changes (made from stage 9 to this stage 11) and then run the app in the emulator to test it.

Commit changes

Click the Commit tab below the Project tab on the left side of the window. Then, mark the "Default Changelist" and "Unversioned Files". Then, enter a commit message i.e. the description of the commit (e.g. Commit done at Stage 11.) (above the commit button) >> click "Commit" (as in Figure 47).

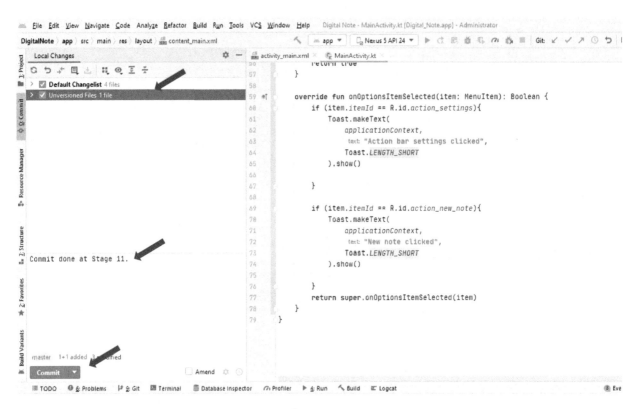

Figure 47

In the dialog box for code analysis, showing info about the number of errors and warnings (as in Figure 48), ignore it and just click "Commit".

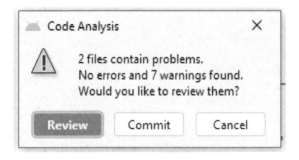

Figure 48

We now have all the files committed. Let us proceed by clicking the 'Project' tab above the 'Commit' tab.

Running the app in our emulator (or Android Virtual Device- AVD)

Next, let us run our app in the emulator.

You can select any of the emulators you already installed in your Android Studio and run the app (as shown in Figure 49).

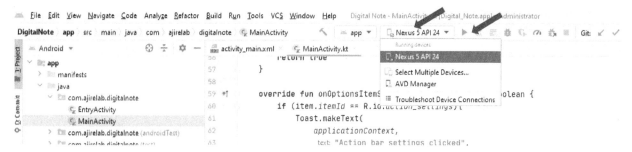

Figure 49

After the launch of your emulator, the Digital Note app should now run successfully as expected (Figure 50).

The first screen you see is for EntryActivity. You can then tap on "OPEN NOTE" to launch the MainActivity. In the screen displayed, you can tap each of the menu items ('Home', 'Settings' and 'Search') in the bottom navigation bar and the options menu hidden in the top action toolbar ('New Note' and 'Settings') to see the toast messages we have coded in them accordingly.

Figure 50

STAGE 12

Implementing CardView and RecyclerView

The CardView file will be referenced by the RecyclerView element which will be inside the content_main.xml

First**, we have to create a layout file for note list item (to be named: item_note_list.xml).** The item_note_list.xml should have CardView added to it.

To create the layout file: go to res >> right-click on 'layout' >> click New >> click Layout Resource File >> let the file name be "item_note_list" and the root element be FrameLayout >> then click OK (as in Figure 51).

Figure 51

For the CardView, we will need vector assets such as ic_assignment and ic_delete (which we have already added to our drawable directory at Stage 4).

Back to our newly created item_note_list.xml. Now let's add CardView, and then, we will add ConstraintLayout. Inside the ConstraintLayout, we need to add an imageView (to hold note icon with an id of ivCardImage), TextView (to hold note category with an id of tvNoteCategory), TextView (to hold note title with an id of tvNoteTitle), imageView (to hold delete icon with an id of ivDelete) and TextView (to hold date of last updated, id = tvLastUpdated).

So, we will update the **item_note_list.xml** as follows:

```xml
<?xml version="1.0" encoding="utf-8"?>
<FrameLayout xmlns:android="http://schemas.android.com/apk/res/android"
xmlns:app="http://schemas.android.com/apk/res-auto"
android:layout_width="match_parent"
android:layout_height="wrap_content">

<androidx.cardview.widget.CardView
    android:layout_width="match_parent"
    android:layout_height="wrap_content"
    app:cardCornerRadius="6dp"
    app:cardElevation="4dp"
    app:cardUseCompatPadding="true"
    app:contentPadding="4dp">

    <androidx.constraintlayout.widget.ConstraintLayout
        android:layout_width="match_parent"
        android:layout_height="wrap_content">

        <ImageView
            android:id="@+id/ivCardImage"
            android:layout_width="wrap_content"
            android:layout_height="wrap_content"
            android:layout_marginStart="8dp"
            android:layout_marginTop="16dp"
            android:tint="@color/my_gold_color"
            app:layout_constraintStart_toStartOf="parent"
            app:layout_constraintTop_toTopOf="parent"
            app:srcCompat="@drawable/ic_assignment"
            android:contentDescription="@string/iv_content_description" />

        <TextView
            android:id="@+id/tvNoteCategory"
            android:layout_width="0dp"
            android:layout_height="wrap_content"
            android:layout_marginStart="8dp"
            android:layout_marginTop="8dp"
            android:layout_marginEnd="16dp"
            android:text="@string/note_category"
            android:textAppearance="@style/TextAppearance.AppCompat.Medium"
            android:textColor="@color/my_gold_color"
            android:textStyle="bold"
            app:layout_constraintEnd_toStartOf="@+id/ivDelete"
            app:layout_constraintStart_toEndOf="@id/ivCardImage"
            app:layout_constraintTop_toTopOf="parent" />

        <TextView
            android:id="@+id/tvNoteTitle"
            android:layout_width="0dp"
            android:layout_height="wrap_content"
            android:layout_marginStart="8dp"
            android:layout_marginTop="5dp"
            android:layout_marginEnd="16dp"
            android:text="@string/note_title"
            android:textAppearance="@style/TextAppearance.AppCompat.Medium"
            android:textSize="18sp"
            app:layout_constraintEnd_toStartOf="@+id/ivDelete"
            app:layout_constraintStart_toEndOf="@id/ivCardImage"
```

```
        app:layout_constraintTop_toBottomOf="@id/tvNoteCategory" />

    <ImageView
        android:id="@+id/ivDelete"
        android:layout_width="wrap_content"
        android:layout_height="wrap_content"
        android:layout_marginTop="16dp"
        android:layout_marginEnd="2dp"
        app:layout_constraintEnd_toEndOf="parent"
        app:layout_constraintTop_toTopOf="parent"
        app:srcCompat="@drawable/ic_delete"
        android:contentDescription="@string/ivdescription_delete_note" />

    <TextView
        android:id="@+id/tvLastUpdated"
        android:layout_width="wrap_content"
        android:layout_height="wrap_content"
        android:layout_marginTop="4dp"
        android:layout_marginEnd="4dp"
        android:layout_marginBottom="4dp"
        android:text="@string/tv_last_updated_date"
        android:textColor="@color/my_accent_color"
        app:layout_constraintBottom_toBottomOf="parent"
        app:layout_constraintEnd_toEndOf="parent"
        app:layout_constraintTop_toBottomOf="@+id/tvNoteTitle" />

    </androidx.constraintlayout.widget.ConstraintLayout>
</androidx.cardview.widget.CardView>
</FrameLayout>
```

For the string references colored in red (that is, @string/iv_content_description, @string/ivdescription_delete_note, and @string/tv_last_updated_date), we will need to update our strings.xml.

So, let us open strings.xml and add the following lines of code:

```
<string name="iv_content_description">Note image icon</string>
<string name="ivdescription_delete_note">Note delete icon</string>
<string name="tv_last_updated_date">Last updated date.</string>
```

Next, we will go back to our item_note_list.xml and switch from code view to design view to see our card view design (as in Figure 52).

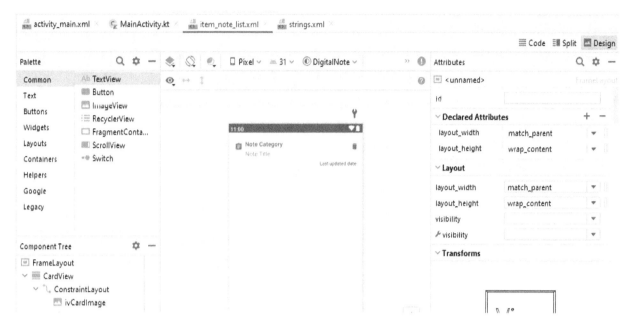

Figure 52

Now that our CardView is ready, we will need to go back to our content_main.xml, and add the RecyclerView with some attributes including id= noteItems and also, we will specifiy "@layout/item_note_list" as the value for "listItem" attribute.

So, let us update our content_main.xml as follows:

```xml
<?xml version="1.0" encoding="utf-8"?>
<androidx.constraintlayout.widget.ConstraintLayout
    xmlns:android="http://schemas.android.com/apk/res/android"
    xmlns:app="http://schemas.android.com/apk/res-auto"
    xmlns:tools="http://schemas.android.com/tools"
    android:layout_width="match_parent"
    android:layout_height="match_parent"
    app:layout_behavior="@string/appbar_scrolling_view_behavior"
    tools:context=".MainActivity"
    tools:showIn="@layout/activity_main">

    <androidx.recyclerview.widget.RecyclerView
        android:id="@+id/noteItem"
        android:layout_width="0dp"
        android:layout_height="0dp"
        android:layout_margin="8dp"
        app:layout_constraintBottom_toBottomOf="parent"
        app:layout_constraintStart_toStartOf="parent"
        app:layout_constraintEnd_toEndOf="parent"
        app:layout_constraintTop_toTopOf="parent"
        tools:listitem="@layout/item_note_list"/>

</androidx.constraintlayout.widget.ConstraintLayout>
```

That's it for the CardView and RecyclerView.

In the content_main.xml, let us switch from Code view to Design view to see the visual of our updates (as in Figure 53).

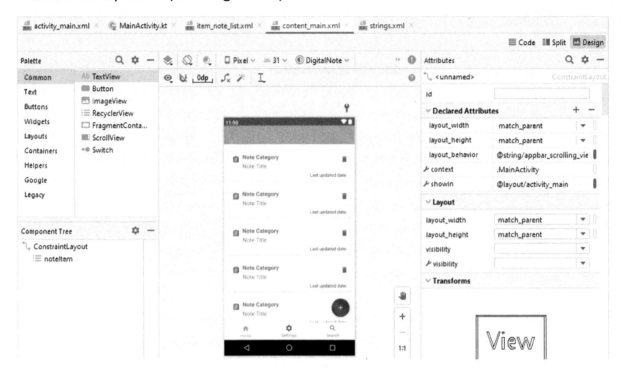

Figure 53

STAGE 13
Addition of New Activity (NoteActivity.kt) from Empty Activity Template

The activity will be for the creation of new notes.

So, we will create a new activity named NoteActivity.

To create the Activity, let us go to File menu >> New >> Activity >> Empty Activity >> Next >> Activity Name: NoteActivity; Ensure that the language is Kotlin >> then click Finish (as in Figure 54).

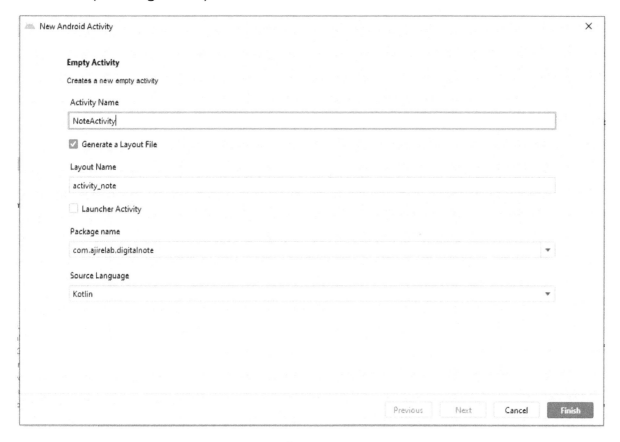

Figure 54

We now have NoteActivity.kt and activity_note.xml.

Updating activity_note.xml

For the activity_note.xml, we will add some more codes to the default codes.

First, we will change the default constraintLayout to **coordinatorLayout**. The codes that we will add will be for the AppBarLayout and its toolbar and the include tag for content_note.xml.

We will add an id to the <include> tag; with the id, we can reference the views in content_note.xml through view binding from NoteActivity.kt.

NB: The content_note in the <include> tag should be in red (that is, layout="@layout/content_note") because it is yet to be created. We will create it in the next stage.

So, let us update the codes in our **activity_note.xml** as follows

```xml
<?xml version="1.0" encoding="utf-8"?>
<androidx.coordinatorlayout.widget.CoordinatorLayout
    xmlns:android="http://schemas.android.com/apk/res/android"
    xmlns:app="http://schemas.android.com/apk/res-auto"
    xmlns:tools="http://schemas.android.com/tools"
    android:layout_width="match_parent"
    android:layout_height="match_parent"
    tools:context=".NoteActivity">

    <!--For App Bar layout-->
    <com.google.android.material.appbar.AppBarLayout
        style="@style/Widget.MaterialComponents.AppBarLayout.PrimarySurface"
        android:layout_width="match_parent"
        android:layout_height="wrap_content"
        android:fitsSystemWindows="true">

        <com.google.android.material.appbar.MaterialToolbar
            android:id="@+id/toolbar"
            style="@style/Widget.MaterialComponents.Toolbar.PrimarySurface"
            android:layout_width="match_parent"
            android:layout_height="?attr/actionBarSize"
            android:elevation="4dp"
            app:layout_scrollFlags="scroll|enterAlways"/>

    </com.google.android.material.appbar.AppBarLayout>

    <include
        android:id="@+id/layout_content_note"
        layout="@layout/content_note" />

</androidx.coordinatorlayout.widget.CoordinatorLayout>
```

STAGE 14
Addition of content_note.xml
(plus commit changes)

We made reference to content_note.xml in activity_note through the <include> tag.

The content_note.xml will contain the main contents that are associated with the NoteActivity.

So, we will go to res >> right-click on layout >> New >> Layout Resource File >> Name = content_note >> OK (as in Figure 55).

Figure 55

So, in **content_note.xml,**, we will add the needed views (a TextView for displaying the date the note was created, a TextView for displaying the date the note was last updated, EditText for note category, Multiline EditText for entering note title, and another Multiline EditText for entering note text, Cancel button and Save Button).

We will add the following to the root element (Constraint Layout).

```
app:layout_behavior="@string/appbar_scrolling_view_behavior"
tools:showIn="@layout/activity_note"
```

Next, we will implement floating label for the EditText views in this content_note.xml using TextInputLayout. This will be achieved by wrapping the EditText views inside the TextInputLayout.

Also, we will limit the number of characters for note category to 50 and that of note title to 90 using android:maxLength attribute.

So, let us update the codes in content_note.xml as follows:

```xml
<?xml version="1.0" encoding="utf-8"?>
<androidx.constraintlayout.widget.ConstraintLayout
xmlns:android="http://schemas.android.com/apk/res/android"
    android:layout_width="match_parent"
    android:layout_height="match_parent"
    xmlns:app="http://schemas.android.com/apk/res-auto"
    xmlns:tools="http://schemas.android.com/tools"
    app:layout_behavior="@string/appbar_scrolling_view_behavior"
    tools:showIn="@layout/activity_note">

    <!--    The app:layout_behavior="@string/appbar_scrolling_view_behavior"
    and tools:showIn="@layout/activity_note" above makes the Action bar to
show properly. Also, it makes the actionbar to be appropriately positioned in
activity_note.xml-->

    <TextView
        android:id="@+id/txvDateCreated"
        android:layout_width="wrap_content"
        android:layout_height="wrap_content"
        android:layout_marginStart="16dp"
        android:layout_marginTop="6dp"
        android:layout_marginEnd="16dp"
        android:text="@string/tv_date_created"
        android:textColor="@color/my_normal_green_color"
        app:layout_constraintEnd_toEndOf="parent"
        app:layout_constraintStart_toStartOf="parent"
        app:layout_constraintTop_toTopOf="parent" />

    <TextView
        android:id="@+id/txvLastUpdated"
        android:layout_width="0dp"
        android:layout_height="wrap_content"
        android:layout_marginStart="16dp"
        android:layout_marginTop="8dp"
        android:layout_marginEnd="16dp"
        android:text="@string/tv_last_updated_date"
        android:textAlignment="center"
        android:textColor="@color/my_accent_color"
        app:layout_constraintEnd_toEndOf="parent"
        app:layout_constraintStart_toStartOf="parent"
        app:layout_constraintTop_toBottomOf="@id/txvDateCreated" />

    <com.google.android.material.textfield.TextInputLayout
        android:layout_width="match_parent"
        android:layout_height="wrap_content"
```

```
        android:id="@+id/layout_noteCategory"
        android:layout_marginStart="16dp"
        android:layout_marginTop="8dp"
        android:layout_marginEnd="16dp"
        app:layout_constraintEnd_toEndOf="parent"
        app:layout_constraintStart_toStartOf="parent"
        app:layout_constraintTop_toBottomOf="@+id/txvLastUpdated">

        <EditText
            android:id="@+id/noteCategory"
            android:layout_width="match_parent"
            android:layout_height="wrap_content"
            android:hint="@string/note_category"
            android:textSize="20sp"
            android:inputType="textMultiLine"
            android:maxLength="50" />
</com.google.android.material.textfield.TextInputLayout>

<com.google.android.material.textfield.TextInputLayout
        android:layout_width="0dp"
        android:layout_height="wrap_content"
        android:id="@+id/layout_textNoteTitle"
        android:layout_marginTop="8dp"
        app:layout_constraintEnd_toEndOf="@+id/layout_noteCategory"
        app:layout_constraintStart_toStartOf="@+id/layout_noteCategory"
        app:layout_constraintTop_toBottomOf="@+id/layout_noteCategory">

        <EditText
            android:id="@+id/textNoteTitle"
            android:layout_width="match_parent"
            android:layout_height="wrap_content"
            android:ems="10"
            android:maxLength="90"
            android:gravity="start|top"
            android:hint="@string/note_title"
            android:inputType="textMultiLine"
            android:textSize="20sp"/>
</com.google.android.material.textfield.TextInputLayout>

<com.google.android.material.textfield.TextInputLayout
        android:layout_width="0dp"
        android:layout_height="wrap_content"
        android:id="@+id/layout_textNoteText"
        android:layout_marginTop="8dp"
        app:layout_constraintEnd_toEndOf="@+id/layout_textNoteTitle"
        app:layout_constraintStart_toStartOf="@+id/layout_textNoteTitle"
        app:layout_constraintTop_toBottomOf="@+id/layout_textNoteTitle">

        <EditText
            android:id="@+id/textNoteText"
            android:layout_width="match_parent"
            android:layout_height="wrap_content"
            android:ems="10"
            android:gravity="start|top"
            android:hint="@string/note_details"
            android:inputType="textMultiLine"
            android:textSize="20sp" />

</com.google.android.material.textfield.TextInputLayout>
```

```xml
<Button
    android:id="@+id/buttonCancel"
    android:layout_width="wrap_content"
    android:layout_height="wrap_content"
    android:layout_marginStart="16dp"
    android:layout_marginTop="16dp"
    android:layout_marginEnd="8dp"
    android:text="@string/cancel"
    android:textStyle="bold"
    android:backgroundTint="@color/my_crimson_color"
    app:layout_constraintEnd_toStartOf="@+id/buttonSave"
    app:layout_constraintHorizontal_bias="0.5"
    app:layout_constraintStart_toStartOf="parent"
    app:layout_constraintTop_toBottomOf="@+id/layout_textNoteText" />

<Button
    android:id="@+id/buttonSave"
    android:layout_width="wrap_content"
    android:layout_height="wrap_content"
    android:layout_marginStart="8dp"
    android:layout_marginTop="16dp"
    android:layout_marginEnd="16dp"
    android:text="@string/save"
    android:backgroundTint="@color/my_normal_green_color"
    android:textStyle="bold"
    app:layout_constraintEnd_toEndOf="parent"
    app:layout_constraintHorizontal_bias="0.5"
    app:layout_constraintStart_toEndOf="@+id/buttonCancel"
    app:layout_constraintTop_toBottomOf="@+id/layout_textNoteText" />

</androidx.constraintlayout.widget.ConstraintLayout>
```

NB: In case the id values are colored in red, simply delete the last letter in the id value and re-enter it to make the red color to turn to green.

Also, for the "@string/tv_date_created", we will need to open our strings.xml and update the codes by adding the following:

```xml
<string name="tv_date_created">Created date.</string>
```

After updating strings.xml, let us go back to content_main.xml and switch from code view to design view (as in Figure 56).

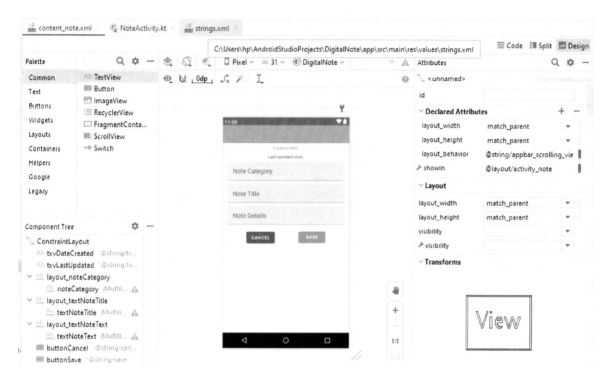

Figure 56

Commit changes

Click the Commit tab below the Project tab on the left side of the window. Then, mark the "Default Changelist" and "Unversioned Files". Then, enter a commit message i.e. the description of the commit (e.g. Commit done at Stage 14.) (above the commit button) > click "Commit" (as in Figure 57).

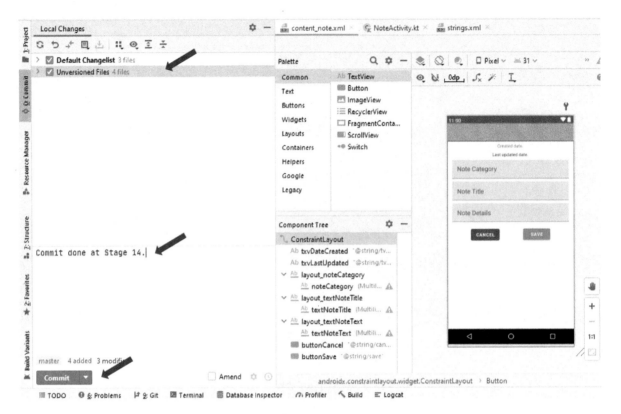

Figure 57

In the dialog box for code analysis, showing info about the number of errors and warnings (as in Figure 58), ignore it and just click "Commit".

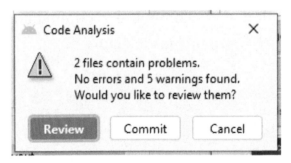

Figure 58

We now have all the files committed. Let us proceed by clicking the 'Project' tab above the 'Commit' tab.

At the next stage, we will work on NoteActivity.kt

STAGE 15
Let's Now Focus on NoteActivity

First, we will need to enable view binding and initialize the toolbar.

For view binding, we will add the following code (to be added above onCreate method)

```
private lateinit var binding: ActivityNoteBinding     // for view
binding for activity_note (a)
```

NB: Press Alt+Enter on ActivityNoteBinding (colored in red) to import it.

Next, we will add the following inside onCreate:

```
binding = ActivityNoteBinding.inflate(layoutInflater)    // for view
binding for activity_note (b)
val view = binding.root                          // for view binding (c)
setContentView(view)                             // for view binding (d)
```

Next, we will add support for toolbar

```
val toolbar = binding.toolbar
setSupportActionBar(toolbar)
```

Next, we will initialize the TextViews and Buttons in content_note.xml

```
val buttonSave = binding.layoutContentNote.buttonSave          //for
initializing and binding save button
val buttonCancel = binding.layoutContentNote.buttonCancel
//for initializing and binding cancel button
val txvLastUpdated = binding.layoutContentNote.txvLastUpdated   //for
initializing and binding last updated textview
val txvDateCreated = binding.layoutContentNote.txvDateCreated   //for
initializing and binding date created textview

//NB: The layoutContentNote was formed by default from the id (i.e.
layout_content_note)that we assigned to the include tag for
content_note.xml
```

Next, we will set the visibility of the TextView with the id- txvLastUpdated to invisible by adding the following code:

```
txvLastUpdated.visibility = View.INVISIBLE
```

NB: We have to press Alt+Enter on the 'View' colored in red to import it.

The txvLastUpdated is to be visible only in EditNoteActivity.kt
So, let us update our NoteActivity.kt as follows:

```
package com.ajirelab.digitalnote

import androidx.appcompat.app.AppCompatActivity
import android.os.Bundle
import com.ajirelab.digitalnote.databinding.ActivityNoteBinding

class NoteActivity : AppCompatActivity() {
    private lateinit var binding: ActivityNoteBinding     // for view binding
for activity_note (a)

    override fun onCreate(savedInstanceState: Bundle?) {
        super.onCreate(savedInstanceState)

        binding = ActivityNoteBinding.inflate(layoutInflater)     // for view
binding for activity_note (b)
        val view = binding.root                      // for view binding (c)
        setContentView(view)                         // for view binding (d)

        val toolbar = binding.toolbar
        setSupportActionBar(toolbar)

        val buttonSave = binding.layoutContentNote.buttonSave          //for
initializing and binding save button
        val buttonCancel = binding.layoutContentNote.buttonCancel
//for initializing and binding cancel button
        val txvLastUpdated = binding.layoutContentNote.txvLastUpdated   //for
initializing and binding last updated textview
        val txvDateCreated = binding.layoutContentNote.txvDateCreated   //for
initializing and binding date created textview

//NB: The layoutContentNote was formed by default from the id (i.e.
layout_content_note) that I assigned to the include tag for content_note.xml

        txvLastUpdated.visibility = View.INVISIBLE
    }
}
```

Next, we will change the App Bar title to "Note Details" from AndroidManifest.

To change the App Bar title, we will go to app >> manifest >> AndroidManifest.xml. Then, we will check the 'label' attribute for the .NoteActivity tag, if not available, we can add it:

```
android:label="@string/note_details"
```

So, in the manifest file, for NoteActivity, we now have:

```
<activity android:name=".NoteActivity"
    android:label="@string/note_details"/>
```

NB: NoteActivity and EditNoteActivity will be using the same layout files (activity_note.xml and content_note.xml). EditNoteActivity.kt will be created as we proceed.

STAGE 16
Coding the fab in MainActivity to Launch NoteActivity when Clicked

We want the Floating Action Button (fab) (as in Figure 59) in MainActivity.kt to navigate us to NoteActivity when clicked or tapped.

```
25        fab.setOnClickListener {   it: View!
26            Toast.makeText( context: this,   text: "New note will be added", Toast.LENGTH_SHORT).show()
27        }
```

Figure 59

So, in the MainActivity.kt, let's modify the code in fab.setOnClickListener, to start NoteActivity by replacing the toast message with the new code as follows:

```
fab.setOnClickListener {
    val intent = Intent(this, NoteActivity::class.java)
    startActivity(intent)
}
```

NB: We have to press Alt+Enter on Intent colored in red to import it.

Running the app

We can now run the app in the emulator and tap the floating action button to add new note (as in Figure 60). We should be navigated to the NoteActivity where new notes can be added.

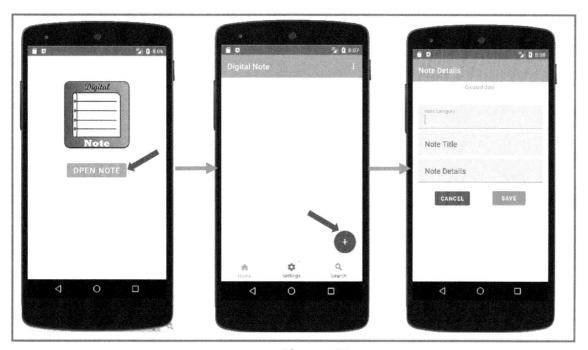

Figure 60

70

STAGE 17
Creation of EditNoteActivity

We will be creating a new activity from Empty Activity template for the Modification of already added notes. In other words, the new activity (to be named EditNoteActivity) will be for handling the editing of notes.

So, to create it, let us go to File >> New >> Activity >> Empty Activity >> Name: EditNoteActivity; **Unmark** "Generate layout file" >> Finish (as in Figure 61). The activity will use the layout files (activity_note.xml and content_note.xml) which are already for NoteActivity.

Figure 61

Next, we will copy the content of NoteActivity.kt and paste in EditNoteActivity.kt. We will then add more codes and make some modifications.

Let us remember that the line of code for setting the visibility of txvLastUpdated to invisible in NoteActivity will not be included in EditNoteActivity because it has to be visible in it.

So, let us update EditNoteActivity.kt as follows:

```
package com.ajirelab.digitalnote

import androidx.appcompat.app.AppCompatActivity
import android.os.Bundle
import com.ajirelab.digitalnote.databinding.ActivityNoteBinding

class EditNoteActivity : AppCompatActivity() {
    private lateinit var binding: ActivityNoteBinding    // for view binding
for activity_note (a)

    override fun onCreate(savedInstanceState: Bundle?) {
        super.onCreate(savedInstanceState)

        binding = ActivityNoteBinding.inflate(layoutInflater)    // for view
binding for activity_note (b)
        val view = binding.root                          // for view binding (c)
        setContentView(view)                             // for view binding (d)
        val toolbar = binding.toolbar
        setSupportActionBar(toolbar)

        val noteCategory = binding.layoutContentNote.noteCategory
//for initializing and binding note category
        val textNoteTitle = binding.layoutContentNote.textNoteTitle
//for initializing and binding note title
        val textNoteText = binding.layoutContentNote.textNoteText
//for initializing and binding note text
        val buttonSave = binding.layoutContentNote.buttonSave          //for
initializing and binding save button
        val buttonCancel = binding.layoutContentNote.buttonCancel
//for initializing and binding cancel button
        val txvLastUpdated = binding.layoutContentNote.txvLastUpdated   //for
initializing and binding last updated textview
        val txvDateCreated = binding.layoutContentNote.txvDateCreated   //for
initializing and binding date created textview

//NB: The layoutContentNote was formed by default from the id (i.e.
layout_content_note) that I assigned to the include tag for content_note.xml
    }
}
```

Next, we will also add label to its tag in AndroidManifest file.

So, let us open AndroidManifest.xml (from app >> manifests >> AnrdroidManifest.xml) and update the tag for EditNoteActivity as follows:

```
<activity android:name=".EditNoteActivity"
    android:label="@string/note_details"/>
```

We now have the EditNoteActivity added and configured to use activity_note.xml and content_note.xml as its layout files.

In the next stage, we will be adding a Kotlin class that will handle the conversion of long to date type and date to long type accordingly. This will be useful for the last updated date.

STAGE 18
Creation of DateTypeConverter.kt Class
(plus commit changes)

In this Kotlin class, we will add the code for type converter that will convert Date to and from Long data type.

To do this, let us go to app >> java >> right-click on the app name >> New >> Kotlin Class/File (as in Figure 62) >> name = DateTypeConverter >> Select Class >> Press Enter (as in Figure 63).

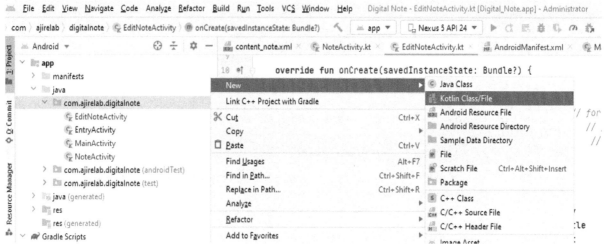

Figure 62

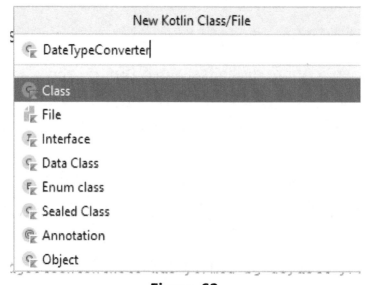

Figure 63

Next, let us update the content of DateTypeConverter.kt as follows:

```kotlin
package com.ajirelab.digitalnote

import androidx.room.TypeConverter
import java.util.*

class DateTypeConverter {
    @TypeConverter
    fun toDate(value: Long?): Date? {
        return if(value == null) null else Date(value)
    }
    @TypeConverter
    fun toLong(value: Date?): Long? {
        return value?.time
    }
}
```

Commit changes

Click the Commit tab below the Project tab on the left side of the window. Then, mark the "Default Changelist" and "Unversioned Files". Then, enter a commit message i.e. the description of the commit (e.g. Commit done at Stage 18.) (above the commit button) >> click "Commit" (as in Figure 64).

Figure 64

In the dialog box for code analysis, showing info about the number of errors and warnings (as in Figure 65), ignore it and just click "Commit".

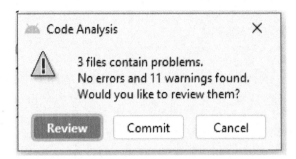

Figure 65

We now have all the files committed. Let us proceed by clicking the 'Project' tab above the 'Commit' tab.

STAGE 19

Setting up the Room Database by adding all necessary classes and files

At this stage, we will be adding some Kotlin classes and files to handle the storage of our data in Room Database. Let us remember that we have already added the dependencies for Room in Stage 2.

1. **Addition of Note.kt (class)**

   In the Note.kt, we will create our table- defined as Entity using the @Entity annotation, and use tableName attribute to define the name of the table.

   Also, we will create columns such as id (to store the id for each note), category (to store note category), title (to store note title), details (to store note details), date_created (to store the date the note was first created) and last_updated (to store the date the note was last updated).

   Note that every table or entity class should have at least a primary key (with @PrimaryKey annotation). In our case, the PrimaryKey will be the id.

   Also note that ColumnInfo attribute (with @ColumnInfo annotation) is used to assign specific name to a column.

   Now, let us go to app >> java >> right-click on the app name (com.ajirelab.digitalnote) >> New >> Kotlin Class/File >> Enter Note as name (as in Figure 66) >> Select Class >> Press Enter.

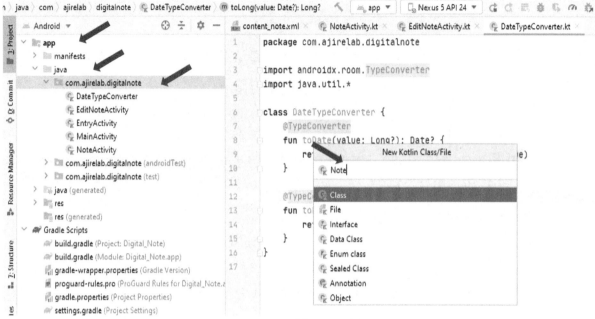

Figure 66

In the Note.kt created, let us update the codes as follows:

```kotlin
package com.ajirelab.digitalnote

import androidx.room.ColumnInfo
import androidx.room.Entity
import androidx.room.PrimaryKey
import java.util.*

@Entity (tableName = "notes")
class Note (@PrimaryKey
           val id: String,
           val category: String,
           val title: String,
           val details: String,

           @ColumnInfo(name = "date_created")
           val dateCreated: String?,

           @ColumnInfo(name = "last_updated")
           val lastUpdated: Date?)
```

2. Addition of NoteDao.kt (interface)

We will now be adding a Dao interface to our room database. Dao stands for Data Access Objects. As the name implies, it provides the methods of accessing the data in the database.

It is in this Dao interface that we will implement the following operations: insert operation using @Insert annotation (to interact with the database by adding data to it), update operation using @Update annotation (to update the data that we have in the database), delete operation using @Delete annotation (to remove data from our database) and query operation using @Query annotation (to locate and retrieve data from the database).

Now, let us go to app >> java >> right-click on the app name (com.ajirelab.digitalnote) >> New >> Kotlin Class/File >> Enter NoteDao as name (as in Figure 67) >> Select Interface >> Press Enter.

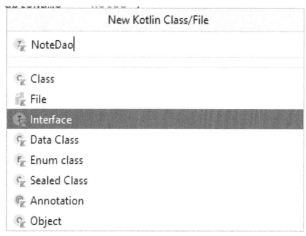

Figure 67

Let us now update the codes in the NoteDao.kt created as follows:

```kotlin
package com.ajirelab.digitalnote

import androidx.lifecycle.LiveData
import androidx.room.*

@Dao
interface NoteDao {
    @Insert
    suspend fun insert(note: Note)

    @get:Query("SELECT * FROM notes")
    val allNotes: LiveData<List<Note>>

    @Update
    suspend fun update(note: Note)

    @Delete
    suspend fun delete(note: Note)
}
```

3. Addition of NoteRoomDatabase.kt (class)

Now, we will be creating a database class for Room. We will name the class NoteRoomDatabase. In it, we will add @Database and @TypeConverters annotations. Also, we will make the class an abstract class that will extend RoomDatabase() superclass.

Next, we will associate the database with our Dao by defining an abstract function for the Dao. Next, we will initialize an instance of the room database using a singleton object.

In the singleton object, we will create a property of noteRoomInstance and define the getDatabase function (which we will use to get the instance of the NoteRoomDatabase).

In the getDatabase function, we will first check if our database instance is null, and if it is null, we will create a new instance for the database. (**NB:** The line with 'synchronized' will be there to ensure that our RoomDatabase is used in a single thread, thereby ensuring thread safety).

So, if the database instance is null, we will initialize it with the new database instance and acquire the instance of the database using the Room.databaseBuilder function. Note that the third parameter in the builder function is the name we would like to use for our database. In our case, we will be using the name- note_database.

At the end of the getDatabase function, the RoomDatabase (that is, noteRoomInstance) is returned. With this, if the database instance is null, a new instance will be created; but if it is not null, the same noteRoomInstance will be returned to the calling function.

Now, let us go to app >> java >> right-click on the app name (com.ajirelab.digitalnote) >> New >> Kotlin Class/File >> Enter NoteRoomDatabase as name >> Select Class >> Press Enter.

NoteRoomDatabase.kt is now created.

Next, let us update the codes in the NoteRoomDatabase.kt created as follows:

```kotlin
package com.ajirelab.digitalnote

import android.content.Context
import androidx.room.Database
import androidx.room.Room
import androidx.room.RoomDatabase
import androidx.room.TypeConverters

@Database(entities = [Note::class], version = 1, exportSchema = false)
@TypeConverters(DateTypeConverter::class)

abstract class NoteRoomDatabase: RoomDatabase() {

    abstract fun noteDao(): NoteDao

    companion object{
        private var noteRoomInstance: NoteRoomDatabase? = null
        fun getDatabase(context: Context): NoteRoomDatabase?{
            if (noteRoomInstance == null) {
                synchronized(NoteRoomDatabase::class.java){
                    if (noteRoomInstance == null){
                        noteRoomInstance =
Room.databaseBuilder(context.applicationContext,
                        NoteRoomDatabase::class.java,
"note_database").build()
                    }
                }
            }
            return noteRoomInstance
        }
    }
}
```

Note that if there is any need for us to write migrations for the purpose of adding more columns to our table, we can get the migrations written here in the NoteRoomDatabase.kt.

4. **Addition of NoteRepository.kt (class)**

Using a repository is considered as one of the best practices when dealing with room database, particularly for organizing data. With the repository, we will have a clean API that could be used by the other parts of the application to access data. It manages queries and provides the opportunity to use multiple backends.

In the repository, we also have the opportunity to decide whether to retrieve data from our local database (like the NoteDao) or from a network.

Our ViewModel(s) will use this NoteRepository to fetch data from the NoteDao.

Now, let us go to app >> java >> right-click on the app name (com.ajirelab.digitalnote) >> New >> Kotlin Class/File >> Enter NoteRepository as name >> Select Class >> Press Enter.

Our NoteRepository.kt is now created.

Next, let us update the codes in the NoteRepository.kt created as follows:

```kotlin
package com.ajirelab.digitalnote
import androidx.lifecycle.LiveData

class NoteRepository(private val noteDao: NoteDao) {

    val allNotes: LiveData<List<Note>> = noteDao.allNotes

    suspend fun insert(note: Note) {
        noteDao.insert(note)
    }

    suspend fun update(note: Note){
        noteDao.update(note)
    }

    suspend fun delete(note: Note){
        noteDao.delete(note)
    }
}
//NB: We used suspend fun because we will be using it with
Coroutines.We have also used the suspend fun in our NoteDao.kt.
```

5. Addition of NoteViewModel.kt (class)

ViewModel helps us to prepare the data for the user interface (UI).

The ViewModel will hold and process our LiveData, and ensure that our app survives configuration changes (such as when the device orientation is changed or when we press the back button). In addition, ViewModel serves as communication layer between the database and the UI.

In the ViewModel class, we will be using Kotlin coroutine to run some background operations that our app requires. Note that we already added the dependencies for Kotlin coroutines in Stage 2.

The 'viewModelScope.launch(Dispatchers.IO)' creates a background coroutine that runs on an IO thread. The IO Dispatchers is used to perform operations such as reading from and writing to the database.

Now, let us go to app >> java >> right-click on the app name (com.ajirelab.digitalnote) >> New >> Kotlin Class/File >> Enter NoteViewModel as name >> Select Class >> Press Enter.

Our NoteViewModel.kt is now created.
Let us update the codes in our NoteViewModel.kt as follows:

```kotlin
package com.ajirelab.digitalnote

import android.app.Application
import androidx.lifecycle.AndroidViewModel
import androidx.lifecycle.LiveData
import androidx.lifecycle.viewModelScope
import kotlinx.coroutines.*

class NoteViewModel(application: Application):
AndroidViewModel(application) {

    val allNotes: LiveData<List<Note>>
    val noteRepository: NoteRepository

    init {
        val dao = NoteRoomDatabase.getDatabase(application)!!.noteDao()
        noteRepository = NoteRepository(dao)
        allNotes = noteRepository.allNotes
    }

    fun insert(note: Note) = viewModelScope.launch(Dispatchers.IO) {
        noteRepository.insert(note)
    }

    fun update(note: Note) = viewModelScope.launch(Dispatchers.IO){
        noteRepository.update(note)
    }

    fun delete(note: Note) = viewModelScope.launch(Dispatchers.IO) {
        noteRepository.delete(note)
    }
}
```

STAGE 20
Addition of NoteRecyclerAdapter Class

In the Adapter class, we will write the codes for binding data to our RecyclerView. We will also add an inner class for our ViewHolder.

Now, let us go to app >> java >> right-click on the app name (com.ajirelab.digitalnote) >> New >> Kotlin Class/File >> Enter NoteRecyclerAdapter as name >> Select Class >> Press Enter.

In the NoteRecyclerAdapter, we will implement view binding, add the inner class, and implement the three methods for the adapter class- that is, onCreateViewHolder method (where we will be setting the view for each of our RecyclerView list items), onBindViewHolder method (where we will be setting the data for each of the items) and the getItemCount method (which will count the data or number of items in the list).

```kotlin
override fun onCreateViewHolder(parent: ViewGroup, viewType: Int):
NoteViewHolder {
    val binding =
ItemNoteListBinding.inflate(LayoutInflater.from(parent.context),
parent, false)
    return NoteViewHolder(binding)
}

inner class NoteViewHolder(val binding: ItemNoteListBinding) :
RecyclerView.ViewHolder(binding.root) {
    private var pos: Int = 0
    fun setData(category: String, title : String, lastUpdated: Date?,
position: Int) {
        binding.tvNoteCategory.text = category
        binding.tvNoteTitle.text = title
        binding.tvLastUpdated.text = getFormattedDate(lastUpdated)

        this.pos = position
    }

binding.ivDelete.setOnClickListener {
    onDeleteClickListener.onDeleteClickListener(noteList[pos])
}
```

So, let us now update the NoteRecyclerAdapter.kt as follows:

```kotlin
package com.ajirelab.digitalnote

import android.app.Activity
import android.content.Context
```

```kotlin
import android.content.Intent
import android.view.LayoutInflater
import android.view.ViewGroup
import androidx.recyclerview.widget.RecyclerView
import com.ajirelab.digitalnote.databinding.ItemNoteListBinding
import java.text.SimpleDateFormat
import java.util.*

class NoteRecyclerAdapter(private val context: Context,
                          private val onDeleteClickListener:
OnDeleteClickListener) :
RecyclerView.Adapter<NoteRecyclerAdapter.NoteViewHolder>() {

    interface OnDeleteClickListener {
        fun onDeleteClickListener(myNote: Note)
    }

    private var noteList: List<Note> = mutableListOf()

    override fun onCreateViewHolder(parent: ViewGroup, viewType: Int):
NoteViewHolder {
        val binding =
ItemNoteListBinding.inflate(LayoutInflater.from(parent.context), parent,
false)
        return NoteViewHolder(binding)
    }

    override fun onBindViewHolder(holder: NoteViewHolder, position: Int) {
        val note = noteList[position]
        holder.setData(note.category, note.title, note.lastUpdated, position)
        holder.setListeners()
    }

    override fun getItemCount(): Int = noteList.size

    fun setNotes(notes: List<Note>) {
        noteList = notes
        notifyDataSetChanged()
    }

    inner class NoteViewHolder(val binding: ItemNoteListBinding) :
RecyclerView.ViewHolder(binding.root) {
        private var pos: Int = 0

        fun setData(category: String, title : String, lastUpdated: Date?,
position: Int) {
            binding.tvNoteCategory.text = category
            binding.tvNoteTitle.text = title
            binding.tvLastUpdated.text = getFormattedDate(lastUpdated)

            this.pos = position
        }

        private fun getFormattedDate(lastUpdated: Date?): String {
            var time = context.getString(R.string.time_last_updated)
            time += lastUpdated?.let {
                val sdf = SimpleDateFormat("HH:mm d MMM, yyyy",
Locale.getDefault())
                sdf.format(lastUpdated)
```

```kotlin
            } ?: "Not found"
            return time
        }

        fun setListeners() {
            itemView.setOnClickListener {
                val intent = Intent(context, EditNoteActivity::class.java)
                intent.putExtra("id", noteList[pos].id)
                intent.putExtra("category", noteList[pos].category)
                intent.putExtra("title", noteList[pos].title)
                intent.putExtra("details", noteList[pos].details)
                intent.putExtra("dateCreated", noteList[pos].dateCreated)
                intent.putExtra("lastUpdated",
getFormattedDate(noteList[pos].lastUpdated))
                (context as Activity).startActivityForResult(intent,
MainActivity.UPDATE_NOTE_ACTIVITY_REQUEST_CODE)
            }

            binding.ivDelete.setOnClickListener {
                onDeleteClickListener.onDeleteClickListener(noteList[pos])
            }
        }

    }
}
```

For the string reference colored in red (that is, R.string.time_last_updated), we need to open our strings.xml (from res >> values >> strings.xml) and update it by adding the following line of code:

```xml
<string name="time_last_updated">Last Updated:\u0020</string>
```

NB: The \u0020 creates an empty space after the colon.

In addition, for the UPDATE_NOTE_ACTIVITY_REQUEST_CODE also colored in red (that is, MainActivity.UPDATE_NOTE_ACTIVITY_REQUEST_CODE), we will need to update our MainActivity.kt accordingly. This will be done in the next stage.

STAGE 21
Update of MainActivity.kt

First, we will initialize the view model:

```
private lateinit var noteViewModel: NoteViewModel
```

Next, we will bind the RecyclerView from content_main layout file in the MainActivity and then reference it with the id "noteItem".

```
val recyclerView = binding.layoutContentMain.noteItem //for
initializing and binding the Recycler view
```

Next, we will create some constants inside companion object (added before the last '}' in the Activity):

```
companion object{
    private const val NEW_NOTE_ACTIVITY_REQUEST_CODE = 1
    const val UPDATE_NOTE_ACTIVITY_REQUEST_CODE = 2
}
```

Next, we will attach the RecyclerView to MainActivity using the recyclerAdapter.

```
//Code for inflating the recyclerView using the
RecyclerViewAdapter
val noteRecyclerAdapter = NoteRecyclerAdapter(this, this)
recyclerView.adapter = noteRecyclerAdapter

//Code for adding layout Manager to the recycler View and
making the latest note to be on the top of the recyclerview.
val myLayoutManager = LinearLayoutManager(this,
LinearLayoutManager.VERTICAL, true)
myLayoutManager.stackFromEnd = true
recyclerView.layoutManager = myLayoutManager
```

NB: We are to press Alt+Enter on the LinearLayoutManager colored in red to import it.

Next, we will declare a private function named 'goToNewNote' as follows:

```
private fun goToNewNote() {
    val intent = Intent(this, NoteActivity::class.java)
    startActivityForResult(intent, NEW_NOTE_ACTIVITY_REQUEST_CODE)
}
```

Since the floating action button and the toolbar menu item (action_new_note) are performing the same function of launching the NoteActivity, we can just call the goToNewNote function inside the 'fab.setOnclickListener' and the 'item.itemid == R.id.action_new_note'

So, we will modify the fab codes as follows:

```
fab.setOnClickListener {
        goToNewNote()
    }
```

Next, we will update the onOptionsItemSelected function. When 'New Note' is tapped, the NoteActivity.kt should be launched. So, we will also call goToNewNote() function.

```
if (item.itemId == R.id.action_new_note){
    goToNewNote()
}
```

Next, we will update the Home bottom menu item in bottomNavView.setOnItemSelectedListener

```
R.id.bottom_nav_home ->
    Toast.makeText(
                applicationContext,
                getString(R.string.toast_you_are_here),
                Toast.LENGTH_SHORT
            ).show()
```

NB: We will later update the strings.xml to resolve the reference colored in red, that is, getString(R.string.toast_you_are_here).

Next, we will initialize the ViewModel (to be done above onCreate)

```
private lateinit var noteViewModel: NoteViewModel
```

Next, we will write the codes for the ViewModel:

```
noteViewModel = ViewModelProvider(this,
ViewModelProvider.AndroidViewModelFactory.getInstance(applicati
on)).get(NoteViewModel::class.java)
noteViewModel.allNotes.observe(this, Observer{notes ->
    notes?.let{
        noteRecyclerAdapter.setNotes(notes)
    }
})
```

NB: Press Alt +Enter on the 'ViewModelProvider' and 'observe' colored in red to import them.

87

Next, we will add NoteRecyclerAdapter.OnDeleteClickListener and then implement its member.

```
class MainActivity : AppCompatActivity(),
NoteRecyclerAdapter.OnDeleteClickListener {
```

To implement its members, we will press Alt+ Enter on MainActivity underlined in red, highlight the members in the box shown and click OK.

We will then update the OnDeleteClickListener implemented accordingly

```
        //Alert Dialog was activated to ensure that users confirm a note
before deletion
        override fun onDeleteClickListener(myNote: Note) {
            val builder = AlertDialog.Builder(this@MainActivity)
            builder.setMessage(getString(R.string.confirm_note_delete))
                .setCancelable(false)
                .setPositiveButton(getString(R.string.yes)) {
                        dialog, id ->
                    noteViewModel.delete(myNote)
                    Toast.makeText(applicationContext,
R.string.note_deleted, Toast.LENGTH_SHORT).show()
                }
                .setNegativeButton(getString(R.string.no)) {
                        dialog, id ->
                    dialog.dismiss()
                }
            val alert = builder.create()
            alert.show()

        }
```

NB: Press Alt + Enter on the AlertDialog colored in red to import it.

For the string references colored in red (that is, R.string.confirm_note_delete, R.string.yes, R.string.no), we will update our strings.xml later.

Next, we will override onResume method.

```
        override fun onResume() {
        super.onResume()
        val recyclerView = binding.layoutContentMain.noteItem   //for
initializing and binding the Recycler view
            recyclerView.adapter?.notifyDataSetChanged()
        }
```

We will also update the strings.xml file
So, in our MainActivity.kt, we should now have:

```
package com.ajirelab.digitalnote

import android.content.Intent
import androidx.appcompat.app.AppCompatActivity
import android.os.Bundle
```

```kotlin
import android.view.Menu
import android.view.MenuItem
import android.widget.Toast
import androidx.appcompat.app.AlertDialog
import androidx.lifecycle.Observer
import androidx.lifecycle.ViewModelProvider
import androidx.recyclerview.widget.LinearLayoutManager
import com.ajirelab.digitalnote.databinding.ActivityMainBinding

class MainActivity : AppCompatActivity(),
NoteRecyclerAdapter.OnDeleteClickListener  {
    private lateinit var binding: ActivityMainBinding    // for view binding
(a)
    private lateinit var noteViewModel: NoteViewModel // for initializing the
ViewModel

    override fun onCreate(savedInstanceState: Bundle?) {
        super.onCreate(savedInstanceState)
        binding = ActivityMainBinding.inflate(layoutInflater) // for view
binding (b)
        val view = binding.root                  // for view binding (c)
        setContentView(view)                     // for view binding (d)

        val toolbar = binding.toolbar     //for initializing and binding the
toolbar
        val fab = binding.fab     ////for initializing and binding the
floating action button
        val bottomNavView = binding.bottomNavView  //for initializing and
binding the bottom navigation view

        val recyclerView = binding.layoutContentMain.noteItem   //for
initializing and binding the Recycler view
        setSupportActionBar(toolbar)

        //Code for inflating the RecyclerView using the RecyclerViewAdapter
        val noteRecyclerAdapter = NoteRecyclerAdapter(this, this)
        recyclerView.adapter = noteRecyclerAdapter

        //Code for adding layout Manager to the recycler View and making the
latest note to be on the top of the Recyclerview.
        val myLayoutManager = LinearLayoutManager(this,
LinearLayoutManager.VERTICAL, true)
        myLayoutManager.stackFromEnd = true
        recyclerView.layoutManager = myLayoutManager

        fab.setOnClickListener {
            goToNewNote()
        }

        noteViewModel = ViewModelProvider(this,
ViewModelProvider.AndroidViewModelFactory.getInstance(application)).get(NoteV
iewModel::class.java)
        noteViewModel.allNotes.observe(this, Observer{notes ->
            notes?.let{
                noteRecyclerAdapter.setNotes(notes)
            }
        })
```

```kotlin
        bottomNavView.setOnItemSelectedListener {
            when(it.itemId) {
                R.id.bottom_nav_home ->
                    Toast.makeText(
                        applicationContext,
                        getString(R.string.toast_you_are_here),
                        Toast.LENGTH_SHORT
                    ).show()

                R.id.bottom_nav_search -> Toast.makeText(
                    applicationContext,
                    "Search clicked",
                    Toast.LENGTH_SHORT
                ).show()

                R.id.bottom_nav_settings -> Toast.makeText(
                    applicationContext,
                    "Settings clicked",
                    Toast.LENGTH_SHORT
                ).show()
            }
            true
        }
    }

    override fun onCreateOptionsMenu(menu: Menu): Boolean {
        // Inflate the menu; this adds items to the action bar if it is
present.
        menuInflater.inflate(R.menu.menu, menu)
        return true
    }

    override fun onOptionsItemSelected(item: MenuItem): Boolean {
        if (item.itemId == R.id.action_settings){
            Toast.makeText(
                applicationContext,
                "Action bar settings clicked",
                Toast.LENGTH_SHORT
            ).show()

        }

        if (item.itemId == R.id.action_new_note){
            goToNewNote()
        }
        return super.onOptionsItemSelected(item)
    }

    private fun goToNewNote() {
        val intent = Intent(this, NoteActivity::class.java)
        startActivityForResult(intent, NEW_NOTE_ACTIVITY_REQUEST_CODE)
    }

    //Alert Dialog was activated to ensure that users confirm a note before
deletion
    override fun onDeleteClickListener(myNote: Note) {
        val builder = AlertDialog.Builder(this@MainActivity)
        builder.setMessage(getString(R.string.confirm_note_delete))
            .setCancelable(false)
```

```
            .setPositiveButton(getString(R.string.yes)) {
                dialog, id ->
                noteViewModel.delete(myNote)
                Toast.makeText(applicationContext, R.string.note_deleted,
Toast.LENGTH_SHORT).show()
            }
            .setNegativeButton(getString(R.string.no)) {
                dialog, id ->
                dialog.dismiss()
            }
        val alert = builder.create()
        alert.show()
    }

    override fun onResume() {
        super.onResume()
        val recyclerView = binding.layoutContentMain.noteItem  //for
initializing and binding the Recycler view
        recyclerView.adapter?.notifyDataSetChanged()
    }

    companion object{
        private const val NEW_NOTE_ACTIVITY_REQUEST_CODE = 1
        const val UPDATE_NOTE_ACTIVITY_REQUEST_CODE = 2
    }

}
```

Updating strings.xml

For the string references colored in red as a result of the updates we made in this Stage 21, we have to update the strings.xml (res >> values >> strings.xml) by adding the lines of code that follows:

```
<string name="toast_you_are_here">You are here!</string>
<string name="confirm_note_delete">Are you sure you want to delete
this note?</string>
<string name="yes">Yes</string>
<string name="no">No</string>
```

STAGE 22
Update of NoteActivity.kt

We will add the following lines of code (to save note when the Save button is tapped and cancel when the Cancel button is tapped) inside onCreate method:

```
buttonSave.setOnClickListener {
    saveNote()
    finish()
}
buttonCancel.setOnClickListener {
    finish()
}
```

Also, we want the note to be saved even when the back button of the device is pressed. So, we will override the onBackPressed method as follows (outside or below onCreate method).

```
//Note will also be saved when the back button of the device is
pressed.
override fun onBackPressed() {
    saveNote()
    super.onBackPressed()
}
```

Next, we will create some constants inside a companion object as follows:

```
companion object{
    const val NEW_CATEGORY = "new_category"
    const val NEW_TITLE = "new_title"
    const val NEW_DETAILS ="new_details"
    const val DATE_CREATED = "date_created"
}
```

Next, we will declare the saveNote() function as follows:

```
private fun saveNote(){
    val resultIntent = Intent()
    if (binding.layoutContentNote.textNoteTitle.text.toString().trim() == ""
&&
        binding.layoutContentNote.textNoteText.text.toString().trim() == ""
){
        setResult(Activity.RESULT_CANCELED, resultIntent)
    }else{
        val category = binding.layoutContentNote.noteCategory.text.toString()
        val title = binding.layoutContentNote.textNoteTitle.text.toString()
        val details = binding.layoutContentNote.textNoteText.text.toString()
        val firstDate =
binding.layoutContentNote.txvDateCreated.text.toString()
```

```
        resultIntent.putExtra(NEW_CATEGORY, category)
        resultIntent.putExtra(NEW_TITLE, title)
        resultIntent.putExtra(NEW_DETAILS, details)
        resultIntent.putExtra(DATE_CREATED, firstDate)
        setResult(Activity.RESULT_OK, resultIntent)
    }
}
```

NB: We have to press Alt+Enter on Intent() and Activity colored in red to import them.

Also, we will add some lines of code for the purpose of formatting the date created and displaying it in the TextView named txvDateCreated (to be added inside onCreate method):

```
//For the purpose of formatting date created.
    val dateTime: String

    val calendar : Calendar = Calendar.getInstance()
    val simpleDateFormat = SimpleDateFormat("dd-MM-yyyy",
Locale.getDefault())
    dateTime = simpleDateFormat.format(calendar.time).toString()
    txvDateCreated.text = getString(R.string.created) + dateTime
```

NB: We will have to press Alt+Enter on Calendar and SimpleDateFormat colored in red to import them.

Also, for the string reference colored in red (that is, R.string.created), we will need to open our strings.xml and add the line of code that follows:

```
<string name="created">Created:\u0020</string>
```

So, in NoteActivity.kt, we have:

```
package com.ajirelab.digitalnote

import android.app.Activity
import android.content.Intent
import androidx.appcompat.app.AppCompatActivity
import android.os.Bundle
import android.view.View
import com.ajirelab.digitalnote.databinding.ActivityNoteBinding
import java.text.SimpleDateFormat
import java.util.*

class NoteActivity : AppCompatActivity() {
    private lateinit var binding: ActivityNoteBinding    // for view binding
for activity_note (a)

    override fun onCreate(savedInstanceState: Bundle?) {
        super.onCreate(savedInstanceState)

        binding = ActivityNoteBinding.inflate(layoutInflater)    // for view
binding for activity_note (b)
        val view = binding.root                            // for view binding (c)
```

```kotlin
        setContentView(view)                        // for view binding (d)

        val toolbar = binding.toolbar
        setSupportActionBar(toolbar)

        val buttonSave = binding.layoutContentNote.buttonSave          //for
initializing and binding save button
        val buttonCancel = binding.layoutContentNote.buttonCancel
//for initializing and binding cancel button
        val txvLastUpdated = binding.layoutContentNote.txvLastUpdated   //for
initializing and binding last updated textview
        val txvDateCreated = binding.layoutContentNote.txvDateCreated   //for
initializing and binding date created textview

//NB: The layoutContentNote was formed by default from the id (i.e.
layout_content_note) that I assigned to the include tag for content_note.xml

        txvLastUpdated.visibility = View.INVISIBLE

        //For the purpose of formatting date created.
        val dateTime: String
        val calendar : Calendar = Calendar.getInstance()
        val simpleDateFormat = SimpleDateFormat("dd-MM-yyyy",
Locale.getDefault())
        dateTime = simpleDateFormat.format(calendar.time).toString()
        txvDateCreated.text = getString(R.string.created) + dateTime

        buttonSave.setOnClickListener {
            saveNote()
            finish()
        }

        buttonCancel.setOnClickListener {
            finish()
        }
    }
    //Note will also be saved when the back button of the device is pressed.
    override fun onBackPressed() {
        saveNote()
        super.onBackPressed()
    }

    private fun saveNote(){
        val resultIntent = Intent()
        if (binding.layoutContentNote.textNoteTitle.text.toString().trim() ==
"" &&
            binding.layoutContentNote.textNoteText.text.toString().trim() ==
"" ){
            setResult(Activity.RESULT_CANCELED, resultIntent)
        }else{
            val category =
binding.layoutContentNote.noteCategory.text.toString()
            val title =
binding.layoutContentNote.textNoteTitle.text.toString()
            val details =
binding.layoutContentNote.textNoteText.text.toString()
            val firstDate =
binding.layoutContentNote.txvDateCreated.text.toString()
```

```kotlin
            resultIntent.putExtra(NEW_CATEGORY, category)
            resultIntent.putExtra(NEW_TITLE, title)
            resultIntent.putExtra(NEW_DETAILS, details)
            resultIntent.putExtra(DATE_CREATED, firstDate)
            setResult(Activity.RESULT_OK, resultIntent)
        }
    }

    companion object{
        const val NEW_CATEGORY = "new_category"
        const val NEW_TITLE = "new_title"
        const val NEW_DETAILS ="new_details"
        const val DATE_CREATED = "date_created"


    }
}
```

STAGE 23
Update of EditNoteActivity.kt

We will first initialize the id variable to null (to be done above onCreate method):

```
var id: String? = null
```

We will then add the following inside onCreate method:

```
val bundle: Bundle? = intent.extras
bundle?.let {
    id = bundle.getString("id")
    val title = bundle.getString("title")
    val category = bundle.getString("category")
    val details = bundle.getString("details")
    val dateCreated = bundle.getString("dateCreated")
    val lastUpdated = bundle.getString("lastUpdated")

    noteCategory.setText(category)
    textNoteTitle.setText(title)
    textNoteText.setText(details)
    txvDateCreated.text = dateCreated
    txvLastUpdated.text = lastUpdated

buttonSave.setOnClickListener{
    updateNote()
    finish()
}

buttonCancel.setOnClickListener {
    finish()
}
}
```

Next, we will add the following lines of code after onCreate method:

```
//Note will also be updated when the back button of the device is pressed.
override fun onBackPressed() {
    updateNote()
    super.onBackPressed()
}

private fun updateNote(){
    val updatedCategory =
binding.layoutContentNote.noteCategory.text.toString()
    val updatedTitle =
binding.layoutContentNote.textNoteTitle.text.toString()
    val updatedDetails =
binding.layoutContentNote.textNoteText.text.toString()
    val dateCreated =
binding.layoutContentNote.txvDateCreated.text.toString()
```

```kotlin
        val resultIntent = Intent()
        resultIntent.putExtra(ID, id)
        resultIntent.putExtra(UPDATED_CATEGORY, updatedCategory)
        resultIntent.putExtra(UPDATED_TITLE, updatedTitle)
        resultIntent.putExtra(UPDATED_DETAILS, updatedDetails)
        resultIntent.putExtra(DATE_CREATED, dateCreated)
        setResult(Activity.RESULT_OK, resultIntent)
    }

    companion object{
        const val ID = "note_id"
        const val UPDATED_CATEGORY = "category_name"
        const val UPDATED_TITLE = "title_name"
        const val UPDATED_DETAILS = "details"
        const val DATE_CREATED = "date_created"
    }
```

NB: We are to press Alt+Enter on the Intent and Activity colored in red to import them.

So, in EditNoteActivity.kt, we have:

```kotlin
package com.ajirelab.digitalnote

import android.app.Activity
import android.content.Intent
import androidx.appcompat.app.AppCompatActivity
import android.os.Bundle
import com.ajirelab.digitalnote.databinding.ActivityNoteBinding

class EditNoteActivity : AppCompatActivity() {

    var id: String? = null

    private lateinit var binding: ActivityNoteBinding     // for view binding
for activity_note (a)

    override fun onCreate(savedInstanceState: Bundle?) {
        super.onCreate(savedInstanceState)

        binding =
            ActivityNoteBinding.inflate(layoutInflater)     // for view binding
for activity_note (b)
        val view = binding.root                      // for view binding (c)
        setContentView(view)                         // for view binding (d)

        val toolbar = binding.toolbar
        setSupportActionBar(toolbar)

        val noteCategory =
            binding.layoutContentNote.noteCategory          //for
initializing and binding note category
        val textNoteTitle =
            binding.layoutContentNote.textNoteTitle          //for
initializing and binding note title
        val textNoteText =
            binding.layoutContentNote.textNoteText          //for
```

97

```kotlin
//initializing and binding note text
        val buttonSave =
            binding.layoutContentNote.buttonSave          //for initializing
and binding save button
        val buttonCancel =
            binding.layoutContentNote.buttonCancel          //for
initializing and binding cancel button
        val txvLastUpdated =
            binding.layoutContentNote.txvLastUpdated   //for initializing and
binding last updated textview
        val txvDateCreated =
            binding.layoutContentNote.txvDateCreated   //for initializing and
binding date created textview

//NB: The layoutContentNote was formed by default from the id (i.e.
layout_content_note)
// that I assigned to the include tag for content_note.xml


        val bundle: Bundle? = intent.extras
        bundle?.let {
            id = bundle.getString("id")
            val title = bundle.getString("title")
            val category = bundle.getString("category")
            val details = bundle.getString("details")
            val dateCreated = bundle.getString("dateCreated")
            val lastUpdated = bundle.getString("lastUpdated")

            noteCategory.setText(category)
            textNoteTitle.setText(title)
            textNoteText.setText(details)
            txvDateCreated.text = dateCreated
            txvLastUpdated.text = lastUpdated

            buttonSave.setOnClickListener {
                updateNote()
                finish()
            }

            buttonCancel.setOnClickListener {
                finish()
            }
        }
    }

    //Note will also be updated when the back button of the device is
pressed.
    override fun onBackPressed() {
        updateNote()
        super.onBackPressed()
    }

    private fun updateNote(){
        val updatedCategory =
binding.layoutContentNote.noteCategory.text.toString()
        val updatedTitle =
binding.layoutContentNote.textNoteTitle.text.toString()
        val updatedDetails =
binding.layoutContentNote.textNoteText.text.toString()
        val dateCreated =
```

```kotlin
binding.layoutContentNote.txvDateCreated.text.toString()

        val resultIntent = Intent()
        resultIntent.putExtra(ID, id)
        resultIntent.putExtra(UPDATED_CATEGORY, updatedCategory)
        resultIntent.putExtra(UPDATED_TITLE, updatedTitle)
        resultIntent.putExtra(UPDATED_DETAILS, updatedDetails)
        resultIntent.putExtra(DATE_CREATED, dateCreated)
        setResult(Activity.RESULT_OK, resultIntent)
    }

    companion object{
        const val ID = "note_id"
        const val UPDATED_CATEGORY = "category_name"
        const val UPDATED_TITLE = "title_name"
        const val UPDATED_DETAILS = "details"
        const val DATE_CREATED = "date_created"
    }
}
```

STAGE 24
Updating the MainActivity by overriding onActivityResult
(plus commit changes and app testing)

In MainActivity.kt, we will override onActivityResult and update the code accordingly. *This could be done above onDeleteClickListener method.*

```kotlin
    override fun onActivityResult(requestCode: Int, resultCode: Int, data:
Intent?) {
        super.onActivityResult(requestCode, resultCode, data)

        if(requestCode == NEW_NOTE_ACTIVITY_REQUEST_CODE && resultCode ==
Activity.RESULT_OK) {
            val id = UUID.randomUUID().toString()
            val categoryName= data?.getStringExtra(NoteActivity.NEW_CATEGORY)
            val titleName = data?.getStringExtra(NoteActivity.NEW_TITLE)
            val details = data?.getStringExtra(NoteActivity.NEW_DETAILS)
            val firstDate = data?.getStringExtra(NoteActivity.DATE_CREATED)
            val currentTime = Calendar.getInstance().time

            val note = Note(id, categoryName!!, titleName!!, details!!,
firstDate, currentTime)

            noteViewModel.insert(note)
            Toast.makeText(applicationContext, R.string.note_saved,
Toast.LENGTH_SHORT).show()

        } else if (requestCode == UPDATE_NOTE_ACTIVITY_REQUEST_CODE &&
resultCode == Activity.RESULT_OK) {
            val id = data?.getStringExtra(EditNoteActivity.ID)
            val categoryName =
data?.getStringExtra(EditNoteActivity.UPDATED_CATEGORY)
            val titleName =
data?.getStringExtra(EditNoteActivity.UPDATED_TITLE)
            val details =
data?.getStringExtra(EditNoteActivity.UPDATED_DETAILS)
            val firstDate = data?.getStringExtra(NoteActivity.DATE_CREATED)
            val currentTime = Calendar.getInstance().time

            val note = Note(id!!, categoryName!!, titleName!!, details!!,
firstDate, currentTime)

            //code to update
            noteViewModel.update(note)
            Toast.makeText(applicationContext, R.string.note_updated,
Toast.LENGTH_SHORT).show()

        }else{
```

```
        Toast.makeText(applicationContext, R.string.not_saved,
Toast.LENGTH_SHORT).show()
        }
    }
```

NB: We will have to press Alt+Enter on Activity, UUID, Calendar colored in red to import them.

Commit changes

Let us commit the changes we have made from Stage 19 to this Stage 24.

Click the Commit tab below the Project tab on the left side of the window. Then, mark the "Default Changelist" and "Unversioned Files". Then, enter a commit message i.e. the description of the commit (e.g. "Commit done at Stage 24. It covers the changes from stage 19 to 24.") (above the commit button) > click "Commit" (as in Figure 68).

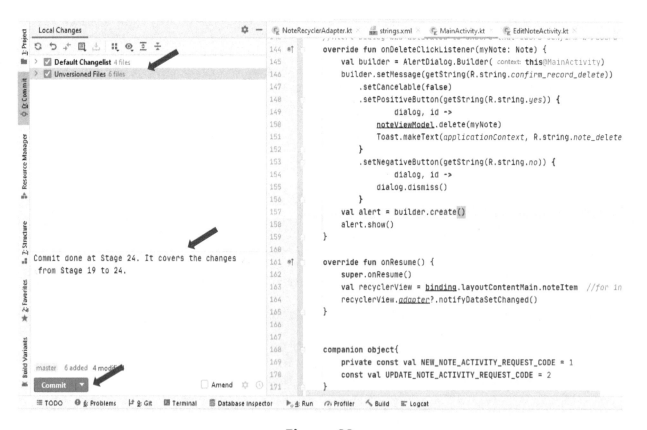

Figure 68

In the dialog box for code analysis, showing info about the number of errors and warnings (as in Figure 69), ignore it and just click "Commit".

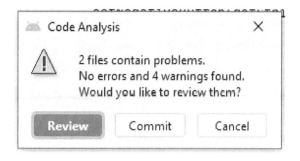

Figure 69

We now have all the files committed. Let us proceed by clicking the 'Project' tab above the 'Commit' tab.

Running the App

Let us run the app in our Emulator to see the progress we have made so far (as in Figure 70). At this stage, we should be able to add, update and delete notes.

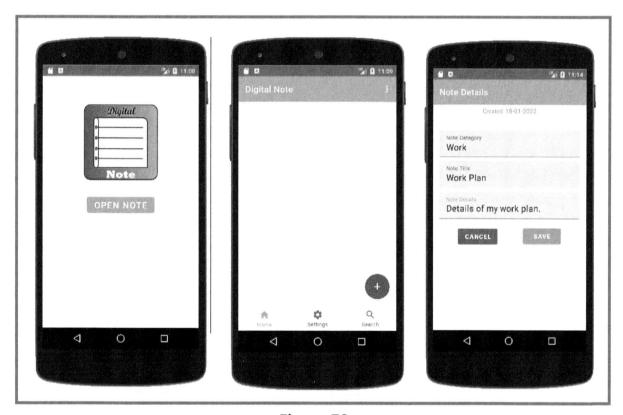

Figure 70a

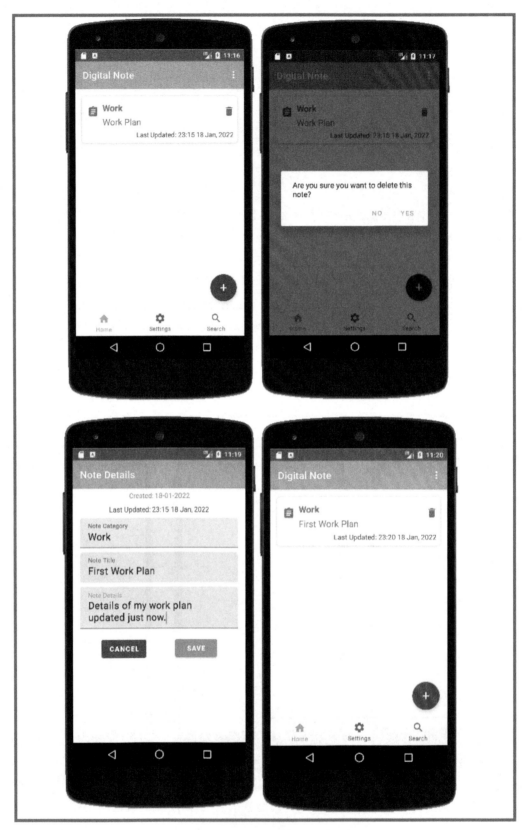

Figure 70b

STAGE 25
Addition of app icon

We already added the image to be used as our app icon to our drawable directory in Stage 4. The name of the image is 'my_app_icon.PNG'.

Let us open AndroidManifest file and set the android icon and android roundIcon to my_app_icon.png. That is,

```
<application
    android:allowBackup="true"
    android:icon="@drawable/my_app_icon"
    android:label="@string/app_name"
    android:roundIcon="@drawable/my_app_icon"
    android:supportsRtl="true"
    android:theme="@style/Theme.DigitalNote">
```

That's it.

The image is now used as app icon.

Let us remember that app icon image should be 512px by 512px.

STAGE 26
Addition of Search Functionality
(plus commit changes and app testing)

With the implementation of search functionality, we should be able to search and locate any note irrespective of the date it was created.

First, we will create new menu resource file named search_menu.xml inside menu directory. To do this, we will go to res >> right-click on menu >> click New >> click Menu Resource File (as in Figure 71).

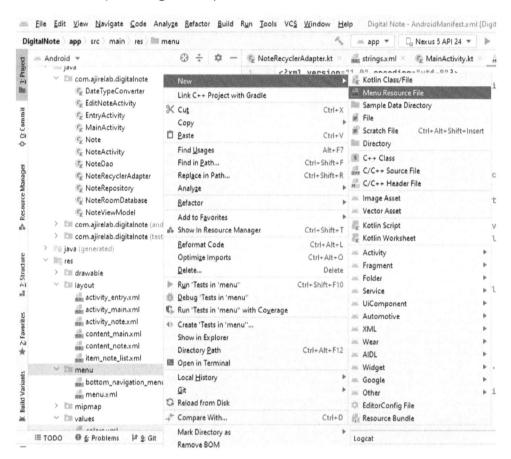

Figure 71

In the dialog box that follows, we will enter 'search_menu' as file name and click OK (as in Figure 72).

Figure 72

In the search_menu.xml file created, we will add a menu item with search icon. Note that we already added the search icon (named "ic_search_white") to our drawable directory in Stage 4. The id of the menu item will be 'searchItems'.

So, let us update the codes in our search_menu.xml as follows:

```xml
<?xml version="1.0" encoding="utf-8" ?>
<menu xmlns:android="http://schemas.android.com/apk/res/android"
    xmlns:app="http://schemas.android.com/apk/res-auto">
    <item android:id="@+id/searchItems"
        android:title="Search"
        android:icon="@drawable/ic_search_white"
        app:showAsAction="ifRoom"

app:actionViewClass="androidx.appcompat.widget.SearchView"/>
</menu>
```

Figure 73 shows how the search menu appears in the Design view

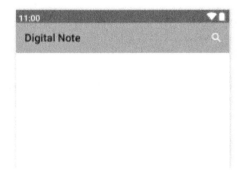

Figure 73

106

Updating NoteDao

Next, we will open NoteDao.kt and add the method for implementing search query.

So, let us update our NoteDao.kt by adding the following lines of code:

```
//The next two lines implement search query. NB: title, category and details
are from Note.kt
@Query("SELECT * FROM notes WHERE title LIKE :desc OR category LIKE :desc OR
details LIKE :desc")
fun getSearchResults(desc: String): LiveData<List<Note>>
```

Updating NoteRepository

Next, we will add a method to NoteRepository.kt as follows:

```
//The next two lines are for implementing the search functionality
@WorkerThread
fun search(desc: String): LiveData<List<Note>>?{
    return noteDao.getSearchResults(desc)
}
```

Creation of SearchViewModel

Next, we will create a ViewModel class named SearchViewModel.kt to handle the search functionality.

To create the view model class, let's go to app >> java >> right-click on the app name (com.ajirelab.digitalnote) >> New >> Kotlin Class/File >> Enter SearchViewModel as name >> Select Class >> Press Enter.

We now have SearchViewModel.kt created.

The contents of SearchViewModel will be slightly similar to that of NoteViewModel. The difference between them is that in SearchViewModel, we did not include the insert function which we included in NoteViewModel. Also, in SearchViewModel, we have added a new method or function (which is absent in NoteViewModel) for searching for items.

So, let us add the following lines of code to update our SearchViewModel.kt

```
package com.ajirelab.digitalnote

import android.app.Application
import androidx.lifecycle.AndroidViewModel
import androidx.lifecycle.LiveData
import androidx.lifecycle.viewModelScope
import kotlinx.coroutines.Dispatchers
import kotlinx.coroutines.launch
```

```kotlin
class SearchViewModel(application: Application):
AndroidViewModel(application) {

    val allNotes: LiveData<List<Note>>
    val noteRepository: NoteRepository

    init {
        val dao = NoteRoomDatabase.getDatabase(application)!!.noteDao()
        noteRepository = NoteRepository(dao)
        allNotes = noteRepository.allNotes
    }

    fun update(note: Note) = viewModelScope.launch(Dispatchers.IO){
        noteRepository.update(note)
    }

    fun delete(note: Note) = viewModelScope.launch(Dispatchers.IO) {
        noteRepository.delete(note)
    }

    fun searchForItems(desc: String) : LiveData<List<Note>>?{
        return noteRepository.search(desc)
    }
}
```

Creation of SearchResultActivity

Next, we will add a new Activity named SearchResultActivity.kt for our Search functionality.

To do this, let us go to File menu >> click New >> click Activity >> click Empty Activity >> Enter SearchResultActivity as Name >> **Unmark** 'Generate a layout file' >> click Finish (as in Figure 74). We have to unmark 'Generate a layout file' because the SearchResultActivity.kt will use the layout of activity_main.xml and content_main.xml that MainActivity is also using.

Figure 74

Next, let us update our new SearchResultActivity by copying some of the codes from MainActivity and pasting in it (because they will have some things in common) and then making some necessary adjustments.

Note that we do not want to have the floating action button for adding new note and the bottom navigation bar displayed in the search screen so, we will set the visibility of the floating action button (fab) to INVISIBLE and bottom navigation view (bottom_nav_view) to GONE.

Let us proceed by updating the codes in our SearchResultActivity.kt as follows.

In SearchResultActivity.kt, we now have:

```
package com.ajirelab.digitalnote

import android.app.Activity
import android.content.Intent
import androidx.appcompat.app.AppCompatActivity
import android.os.Bundle
import android.view.Menu
import android.view.View
import android.widget.Toast
import androidx.appcompat.app.AlertDialog
import androidx.lifecycle.Observer
import androidx.lifecycle.ViewModelProvider
import androidx.preference.PreferenceManager
import androidx.recyclerview.widget.LinearLayoutManager
```

```kotlin
import com.ajirelab.digitalnote.databinding.ActivityMainBinding
import java.util.*


class SearchResultActivity : AppCompatActivity(),
NoteRecyclerAdapter.OnDeleteClickListener  {

    private lateinit var binding: ActivityMainBinding    // for view binding
initialization(a)
    private lateinit var searchViewModel: SearchViewModel   //Code for
initializing the search view model (a)
    private var noteRecyclerAdapter: NoteRecyclerAdapter? = null   //for
noteRecyclerAdapter (a) we initialized it and set its value to null.

    override fun onCreate(savedInstanceState: Bundle?) {
        super.onCreate(savedInstanceState)
        binding = ActivityMainBinding.inflate(layoutInflater)   // for view
binding (b)
        val view = binding.root                          // for view binding (c)
        setContentView(view)                             // for view binding (d)

        val toolbar = binding.toolbar     //for initializing and binding the
toolbar
        val fab = binding.fab      ////for initializing and binding the
floating action button
        val bottomNavView = binding.bottomNavView   //for initializing and
binding the bottom navigation view

        val recyclerView = binding.layoutContentMain.noteItem   //for
initializing and binding the Recycler view

        setSupportActionBar(toolbar)
        supportActionBar?.setDisplayHomeAsUpEnabled(true) //This makes the
back icon to show on the Action bar

        //Code for inflating the recyclerView using the RecyclerViewAdapter
        noteRecyclerAdapter = NoteRecyclerAdapter(this, this) //for
noteRecyclerAdapter (b)
        recyclerView.adapter = noteRecyclerAdapter

        //Code for adding layout Manager to the recycler View and making the
latest note to be on the top of the recyclerview.
        val myLayoutManager = LinearLayoutManager(this,
LinearLayoutManager.VERTICAL, true)
        myLayoutManager.stackFromEnd = true
        recyclerView.layoutManager = myLayoutManager

        fab.visibility = View.INVISIBLE    // this was added to make the fab
button in activity_main.xml invisible in SearchResultActivity
        bottomNavView.visibility = View.GONE // this was added to make the
bottom navigation bar in activity_main.xml invisible and without taking any
space in SearchResultActivity

        //code for initializing the searchViewModel   (b)
        searchViewModel = ViewModelProvider(this,

ViewModelProvider.AndroidViewModelFactory.getInstance(application)).get(Searc
hViewModel::class.java
        )
```

```kotlin
    }

    override fun onCreateOptionsMenu(menu: Menu): Boolean {
        // Inflate the menu; this adds items to the action bar  and then
activates the search menu to work
        menuInflater.inflate(R.menu.search_menu, menu)
        val search = menu.findItem(R.id.searchItems)
        val searchView = search.actionView as
androidx.appcompat.widget.SearchView
        searchView.isSubmitButtonEnabled = true

        //After entering the line next to this comment, I pressed Alt + Enter
on 'object' and then selected to implement its members.
        //Then, the onQueryTextSubmit and onQueryTextChange overrides were
added. I then added some codes into them.
        searchView.setOnQueryTextListener(object :
androidx.appcompat.widget.SearchView.OnQueryTextListener{
            override fun onQueryTextSubmit(query: String?): Boolean {
                if (query != null){
                    getItemsFromDb(query)
                }
                return true
            }
            override fun onQueryTextChange(newText: String?): Boolean {
                if (newText != null){
                    getItemsFromDb(newText)
                }
                return true
            }
        })
        return true
    }

    //The getItemFromDb function below was called inside the
onCreateOptionsmenu above
    //The function is part of the code to handle the search functionality

    private fun getItemsFromDb(searchText: String) {
        var searchText = searchText
        searchText = "%$searchText%"
        searchViewModel.searchForItems(desc = searchText)?.observe(this,
Observer {notes ->
            notes?.let { noteRecyclerAdapter!!.setNotes(notes) }
        })
    }

    // The codes below are to handle the updating of the notes directly from
this SearchResultActivity.
    override fun onActivityResult(requestCode: Int, resultCode: Int, data:
Intent?) {
        super.onActivityResult(requestCode, resultCode, data)
        if (requestCode == UPDATE_NOTE_ACTIVITY_REQUEST_CODE && resultCode ==
Activity.RESULT_OK) {
            val id = data?.getStringExtra(EditNoteActivity.ID)
            val categoryName =
data?.getStringExtra(EditNoteActivity.UPDATED_CATEGORY)
            val titleName =
data?.getStringExtra(EditNoteActivity.UPDATED_TITLE)
            val details =
```

```kotlin
data?.getStringExtra(EditNoteActivity.UPDATED_DETAILS)
            val firstDate = data?.getStringExtra(NoteActivity.DATE_CREATED)
            val currentTime = Calendar.getInstance().time

            val note = Note(id!!, categoryName!!, titleName!!, details!!,
firstDate, currentTime)

            //code to update
            searchViewModel.update(note)
            Toast.makeText(applicationContext, R.string.note_updated,
Toast.LENGTH_SHORT).show()

        }else{
            Toast.makeText(applicationContext, R.string.not_saved,
Toast.LENGTH_SHORT).show()
        }
    }
    //The codes in the onDeleteClickListener below handles the deletion of
notes right from the SearchResultActivity
    //Alert Dialog was activated to ensure that users confirm a note before
deletion
    override fun onDeleteClickListener(myNote: Note) {
        val builder = AlertDialog.Builder(this)
        builder.setMessage(getString(R.string.confirm_note_delete))
            .setCancelable(false)
            .setPositiveButton(getString(R.string.yes)) {
                dialog, id ->
                searchViewModel.delete(myNote)
                Toast.makeText(applicationContext, R.string.note_deleted,
                    Toast.LENGTH_SHORT).show()
            }
            .setNegativeButton(getString(R.string.no)) {
                dialog, id ->
                dialog.dismiss()
            }
        val alert = builder.create()
        alert.show()
    }

    companion object{
        const val UPDATE_NOTE_ACTIVITY_REQUEST_CODE = 2
    }
}
```

Updating MainActivity.kt

In MainActivity.kt, we will write the code to navigate to SearchResultActivity when the Search option menu from the Bottom Navigation Bar is clicked or tapped. So, let us add the following lines of code.

```kotlin
R.id.bottom_nav_search -> goToSearchResultActivity()

private fun goToSearchResultActivity() {
    startActivity(Intent(this, SearchResultActivity::class.java))
}
```

Updating AndroidManifest file

Next, we will go to our AndroidManifest.xml and locate the tag for SearchResultActivity.

We will then add the label to the toolbar and parentActivityName (for navigation to MainActivity when the back icon in the action toolbar is pressed).

So, let us update the AndroidManifest.xml as follows:

```
<activity
    android:name=".SearchResultActivity"
    android:label="@string/search_note"
    android:parentActivityName=".MainActivity" />
```

For the string reference colored in red, we will need to update our string resource file.

Updating strings.xml

So, let us add the line of code that follows to strings.xml

```
<string name="search_note">Search</string>
```

That's it about adding search functionality.

Commit changes

Now, we will commit the changes we have made from Stage 25 to this Stage 26.

Click the Commit tab below the Project tab on the left side of the window. Then, mark the "Default Changelist" and "Unversioned Files". Then, enter a commit message i.e. the description of the commit (e.g. "Commit done at Stage 26.") (above the commit button) > click "Commit".

In the dialog box for code analysis, showing info about the number of errors and warnings, ignore it and just click "Commit".

We now have all the files committed. Let us proceed by clicking the 'Project' tab above the 'Commit' tab.

Running the app

At this stage, let us run the app in our emulator to check how our search functionality works. It works as we expected.

STAGE 27
Addition of Settings functionalities
(plus commit changes and app testing)

At this stage, we will be adding the settings functionality. From the settings screen, we want to be able to switch the background color of the home screen from white to gold colour, and also to be able to enable security so that a password will be required before the note could be opened. In addition, from the settings screen, we should be able to see some information about the app.

The main library we will be using to implement this settings functionality is the Kotlin Preference library, which was already added at Stage 2.

Note that we already have the Settings menu at the bottom navigation bar and also at the action toolbar. In addition, note that the id for the settings menu item is action_settings inside menu.xml.

Also note that we have already inflated the menu in the MainActivity.kt in Stage 11 using the lines of code that follows.

```kotlin
override fun onCreateOptionsMenu(menu: Menu): Boolean {
    // Inflate the menu; this adds items to the action bar if it is
present.
    menuInflater.inflate(R.menu.menu, menu)
    return true
}
```

Creating SettingsActivity.kt

We need to create a new activity named SettingsActivity for settings screen.

To do this, we will go to app >> java >> right-click on the package name >> New >> Activity >> Empty Activity >> Enter SettingsActivity as Name; Mark 'Generate Layout File'. >> click 'Finish' (as in Figure 75).

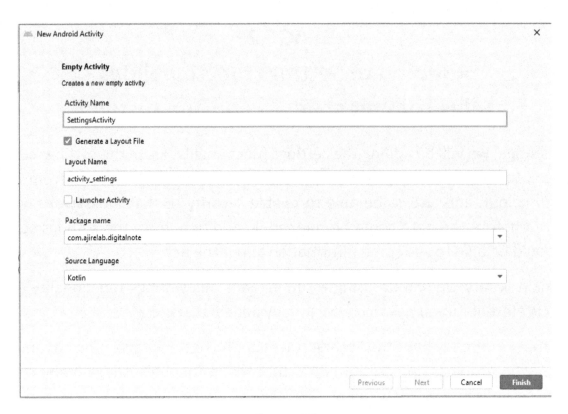

Figure 75

Updating MainActivity.kt

Next, we need to go back to the MainActivity and update the code to handle settings menu item click event.

To do this, let's first create a private function below the goToSearchResultActivity function.

```kotlin
private fun goToSettingsActivity() {
    startActivity(Intent(this, SettingsActivity::class.java))
}
```

Next, we will replace the toast associated with action_settings inside onOptionsItemSelected to a call of the goToSettingsActivity function as follows:

```kotlin
if (item.itemId == R.id.action_settings){
    goToSettingsActivity()
}
```

We will also delete the Toast associated with bottom_nav_settings and call the function to navigate to the Settings screen from the bottom navigation 'settings' item inside bottomNavView.setOnItemSelectedListener.

```kotlin
R.id.bottom_nav_settings -> goToSettingsActivity()
```

Implementing PreferenceScreen

Next, we will need to implement PreferenceScreen for the Settings.

We will first add a xml directory to res by right-clicking on res >> click New >> Android Resource Directory >> Enter 'xml' as Directory name and also select 'xml' as Resource type >> click 'OK' (as in Figure 76).

Figure 76

Next, we will add a xml resource file to the new xml directory. To do this, we will go to 'res' >> right-click on xml >> click New >> XML Resource file >> Enter "preference_settings" as File name >> The Root element should be 'PreferenceScreen' >> click 'OK' (as in Figure 77).

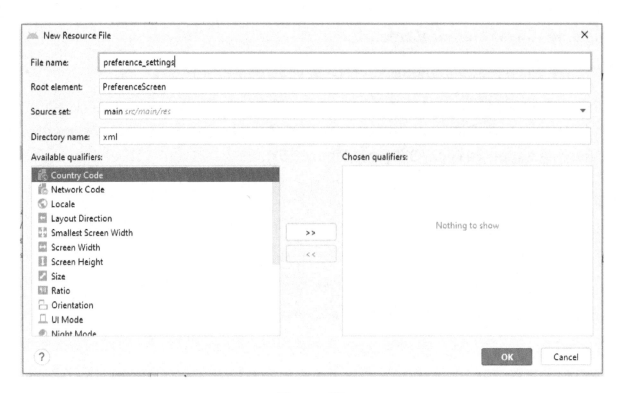

Figure 77

We now have preference_settings.xml created.

Now, inside the preference_settings.xml, we can start adding our preferences using the preference tag. Also, we can use PreferenceCategory tag to put our preferences in categories.

Let us now add our codes and update the preference_settings.xml as follows:

```xml
<?xml version="1.0" encoding="utf-8"?>
<PreferenceScreen
xmlns:android="http://schemas.android.com/apk/res/android"
    xmlns:app="http://schemas.android.com/apk/res-auto">

    <PreferenceCategory
        android:title="@string/prefcat_general"
        app:iconSpaceReserved="false">

        <SwitchPreferenceCompat
            android:defaultValue="false"
            android:key="key_gold_background"
            android:summary="@string/swpref_summary"
            android:title="@string/swpref_title"
            app:iconSpaceReserved="false" />
    </PreferenceCategory>

    <PreferenceCategory
        android:title="@string/prefcat_security"
        app:iconSpaceReserved="false">
```

117

```xml
    <CheckBoxPreference
        android:defaultValue="false"
        android:key="key_secure"
        android:title="@string/ckpref_security_title"
       android:summaryOn="@string/ckpref_security_summary"
        app:iconSpaceReserved="false"  />

    <EditTextPreference
        android:dependency="key_secure"
        android:defaultValue="@string/edpref_default_password"
        android:dialogTitle="@string/edpref_dialog_password"
        android:key="key_password"
        android:title="@string/edpref_title_password"
        app:iconSpaceReserved="false"
        android:inputType="textPassword"
        android:imeOptions="flagNoExtractUi"/>

    <EditTextPreference
        android:dependency="key_secure"
        android:defaultValue=""
        android:dialogTitle="@string/edpref_dialog_question"
        android:key="key_security_question"
        android:title="@string/edpref_title_question"
        app:iconSpaceReserved="false"
        android:inputType="textPassword"
        android:imeOptions="flagNoExtractUi"/>

</PreferenceCategory>

<PreferenceCategory
    android:title="@string/prefcat_about"
    app:iconSpaceReserved="false">

    <Preference
        android:key="key_version"
        android:summary="@string/pref_version_summary"
        android:title="@string/pref_version"
        app:iconSpaceReserved="false"  />

    <Preference
        android:key="key_developer"
        android:title="@string/pref_developer"
        android:summary="@string/pref_developer_summary"
        app:iconSpaceReserved="false"/>

    <Preference
        android:key="key_storage"
        android:title="@string/pref_storage_title"
        android:summary="@string/pref_storage_summary"
        app:iconSpaceReserved="false"/>
</PreferenceCategory>
</PreferenceScreen>
```

For the string references colored in red, we will need to update our strings.xml.

Updating strings.xml

So, let us open strings.xml and add the following lines of code to update it.

```xml
<string name="prefcat_general">General</string>
<string name="swpref_summary">Change home background color to gold.</string>
<string name="swpref_title">Home Background</string>

<string name="prefcat_security">Security</string>
<string name="ckpref_security_title">Require password to open note.</string>
<string name="ckpref_security_summary">Set password and answer security question.</string>
<string name="edpref_title_password">Set a password</string>
<string name="edpref_default_password">****</string>
<string name="edpref_dialog_password">Change password</string>
<string name="edpref_title_question">Answer a security question</string>
<string name="edpref_dialog_question">What is your best hobby?</string>

<string name="prefcat_about">About</string>
<string name="pref_version">Version</string>
<string name="pref_version_summary">1.0 (Released: 2022)</string>
<string name="pref_developer">Developer</string>
<string name="pref_developer_summary">Joseph Ajireloja</string>
<string name="pref_storage_title">Storage</string>
<string name="pref_storage_summary">The notes are stored locally on device memory.</string>
```

Now that our preferences are ready in the preference_settings.xml, we can proceed to link it with our Activity. We will now move to our SettingsActivity.kt and activity_settings.xml.

Updating the activity_settings.xml

In activity_settings.xml, let's first include a toolbar by adding the following lines of code

```xml
<!--This is the code for adding the toolbar app action bar to the activity.-->
    <com.google.android.material.appbar.AppBarLayout
        style="@style/Widget.MaterialComponents.AppBarLayout.PrimarySurface"
        android:id="@+id/appBarLayout"
        android:layout_width="match_parent"
        android:layout_height="wrap_content"
        app:layout_constraintTop_toTopOf="parent"
        app:layout_constraintEnd_toEndOf="parent"
        app:layout_constraintStart_toStartOf="parent"
        android:fitsSystemWindows="true">

        <com.google.android.material.appbar.MaterialToolbar
            android:id="@+id/toolbar"
            style="@style/Widget.MaterialComponents.Toolbar.PrimarySurface"
            android:layout_width="match_parent"
```

```
        android:layout_height="?attr/actionBarSize"
        android:elevation="4dp"
        app:layout_scrollFlags="scroll|enterAlways"/>
    </com.google.android.material.appbar.AppBarLayout>
```

Let us note that the AppBarLayout housing the toolbar has also been assigned an id of "appBarLayout".

Updating SettingsActivity.kt

Next, we will go to SettingsActivity.kt and enable view binding and then initialize the toolbar

```
class SettingsActivity : AppCompatActivity() {
    private lateinit var binding: ActivitySettingsBinding // for view
binding (a)

    override fun onCreate(savedInstanceState: Bundle?) {
        super.onCreate(savedInstanceState)
        binding = ActivitySettingsBinding.inflate(layoutInflater) //
for view binding (b)
        val view = binding.root                    // for view binding (c)
        setContentView(view)                       // for view binding (d)

        val toolbar = binding.toolbar      //for initializing and
binding the toolbar
        setSupportActionBar(toolbar)
    }
}
```

NB: We need to press Alt+Enter on ActivitySettingsBinding colored in red to import it.

Next, we will open AndroidManifest.xml file and add the label for the SettingsActivity.

Updating AndroidManifest.xml

Let us open our AndroidManifest.xml and update it by modifying the tag for SettingsActivity as follows:

```
<activity android:name=".SettingsActivity"
    android:label="@string/settings"
    android:parentActivityName=".MainActivity"/>
```

We have now added a label to the settings screen and added the code to redirect to MainActivity when the back icon is clicked from the action toolbar.

For the string reference colored in red, we will need to update our strings.xml.

Updating strings.xml

So, let us add the following line of code to our strings.xml to update it.

```xml
<string name="settings">Settings</string>
```

Linking Preference Settings with activity_settings.xml and SettingsActivity.kt

In activity_settings.xml, let's add a FrameLayout with an id of 'preference_content' as follows:

```xml
<FrameLayout
    android:id="@+id/preference_content"
    android:layout_width="match_parent"
    android:layout_height="0dp"
    app:layout_constraintBottom_toBottomOf="parent"
    app:layout_constraintEnd_toEndOf="parent"
    app:layout_constraintStart_toStartOf="parent"
    app:layout_constraintTop_toBottomOf="@id/appBarLayout">
</FrameLayout>
```

So, in activity_settings.xml, we now have:

```xml
<?xml version="1.0" encoding="utf-8" ?>
<androidx.constraintlayout.widget.ConstraintLayout
xmlns:android="http://schemas.android.com/apk/res/android"
    xmlns:app="http://schemas.android.com/apk/res-auto"
    xmlns:tools="http://schemas.android.com/tools"
    android:layout_width="match_parent"
    android:layout_height="match_parent"
    tools:context=".SettingsActivity">
    <!--    This is the code for adding the toolbar app action bar to the
activity. -->
    <com.google.android.material.appbar.AppBarLayout
        style="@style/Widget.MaterialComponents.AppBarLayout.PrimarySurface"
        android:id="@+id/appBarLayout"
        android:layout_width="match_parent"
        android:layout_height="wrap_content"
        app:layout_constraintTop_toTopOf="parent"
        app:layout_constraintEnd_toEndOf="parent"
        app:layout_constraintStart_toStartOf="parent"
        android:fitsSystemWindows="true">

        <com.google.android.material.appbar.MaterialToolbar
            android:id="@+id/toolbar"
            style="@style/Widget.MaterialComponents.Toolbar.PrimarySurface"
            android:layout_width="match_parent"
            android:layout_height="?attr/actionBarSize"
            android:elevation="4dp"
            app:layout_scrollFlags="scroll|enterAlways"/>
    </com.google.android.material.appbar.AppBarLayout>
```

```
<FrameLayout
    android:id="@+id/preference_content"
    android:layout_width="match_parent"
    android:layout_height="0dp"
    app:layout_constraintBottom_toBottomOf="parent"
    app:layout_constraintEnd_toEndOf="parent"
    app:layout_constraintStart_toStartOf="parent"
    app:layout_constraintTop_toBottomOf="@id/appBarLayout">
</FrameLayout>

</androidx.constraintlayout.widget.ConstraintLayout>
```

Updating SettingsActivity.kt

Next, we will move to SettingsActivity.kt and get some work done there.

Inside its onCreate method, we will enter the following lines of code:

```
if(savedInstanceState == null){
    supportFragmentManager
        .beginTransaction()
        .replace(R.id.preference_content, SettingsPreference())
    //The preference_content is located in activity_settings.xml
    while the SettingsPreference is the class newly created below.
        .commit()
}
```

Next, outside or below onCreate method, we will create a class for SettingsPreference and extend PreferenceFragmentCompat, and then press Alt+Enter on 'SettingsPreference' to implement members as in Figure 78.

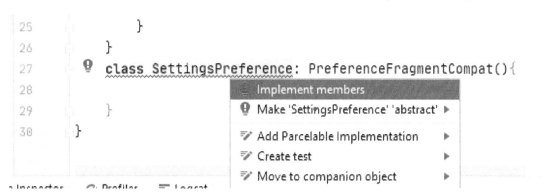

Figure 78

After deleting the TODO line and implementing the members, we should now have the lines of code that follows:

```
class SettingsPreference: PreferenceFragmentCompat(){
    override fun onCreatePreferences(savedInstanceState: Bundle?,
```

```
rootKey: String?) {

    }
}
```

Inside the member added (that is the onCreatePreferences method, we will set preferences from resource by updating the code as follows:

```
class SettingsPreference : PreferenceFragmentCompat(){
    override fun onCreatePreferences(savedInstanceState: Bundle?,
rootKey: String?) {
        setPreferencesFromResource(R.xml.preference_settings,
rootKey)
    }
}
```

Next, in the SettingsActivity class, we will extend

```
SharedPreferences.OnSharedPreferenceChangeListener
```

That is,

```
class SettingsActivity : AppCompatActivity(),
SharedPreferences.OnSharedPreferenceChangeListener{
```

We will then press Alt + Enter on SettingsActivity (underlined in red) and then implement its members as in Figure 79.

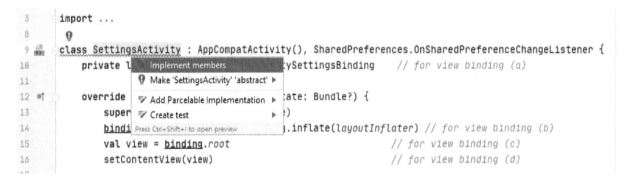

Figure 79

After implementing its members, we now have onSharedPreferenceChanged method added to our code as in Figure 80.

123

```
 8
 9    class SettingsActivity : AppCompatActivity(), SharedPreferences.OnSharedPreferenceChangeListener {
10        private lateinit var binding: ActivitySettingsBinding    // for view binding (a)
11
12    •↑    override fun onCreate(savedInstanceState: Bundle?) {
13            super.onCreate(savedInstanceState)
14            binding = ActivitySettingsBinding.inflate(layoutInflater) // for view binding (b)
15            val view = binding.root                        // for view binding (c)
16            setContentView(view)                           // for view binding (d)
17            val toolbar = binding.toolbar    //for initializing and binding the toolbar
18            setSupportActionBar(toolbar)
19
20            if(savedInstanceState == null){
21                supportFragmentManager
22                    .beginTransaction()
23                    .replace(R.id.preference_content, SettingsPreference()) //The preference_content is located
24                    .commit()
25            }
26        }
27        class SettingsPreference: PreferenceFragmentCompat(){
28    •↑        override fun onCreatePreferences(savedInstanceState: Bundle?, rootKey: String?) {
29                setPreferencesFromResource(R.xml.preference_settings, rootKey)
30            }
31        }
32
33    •↑    override fun onSharedPreferenceChanged(p0: SharedPreferences?, p1: String?) {
34            TODO( reason: "Not yet implemented")
35        }
36    }
```

Figure 80

Now, we will delete the line for TODO and then change p0 to sharedPreferences
and p1 to key as follows:

```
override fun onSharedPreferenceChanged(sharedPreferences:
SharedPreferences?, key: String?) {

}
```

Next, inside onCreate method, we will enter the following lines of code:

```
PreferenceManager.getDefaultSharedPreferences(this)
    .registerOnSharedPreferenceChangeListener(this)
```

NB: We will press Alt+Enter on PreferenceManager colored in red to import it.

Next, we will declare a function that will contain the lines of code for setting up our
toolbar and then call the function inside onCreate method.

So, outside onCreate method, let's declare the function as follows:

```kotlin
private fun setUpToolbar() {
    supportActionBar?.setDisplayHomeAsUpEnabled(true)
    supportActionBar?.setDisplayShowHomeEnabled(true)
}
```

Then, we will call the function inside onCreate method by adding the following line of code:

```kotlin
setUpToolbar() //This function is called to setup the toolbar
```

That's it.

In our SettingsActivity.kt, our codes should have now been updated to:

```kotlin
package com.ajirelab.digitalnote

import android.content.SharedPreferences
import androidx.appcompat.app.AppCompatActivity
import android.os.Bundle
import androidx.preference.PreferenceFragmentCompat
import androidx.preference.PreferenceManager
import com.ajirelab.digitalnote.databinding.ActivitySettingsBinding

class SettingsActivity : AppCompatActivity(),
SharedPreferences.OnSharedPreferenceChangeListener {
    private lateinit var binding: ActivitySettingsBinding      // for view
binding (a)

    override fun onCreate(savedInstanceState: Bundle?) {
        super.onCreate(savedInstanceState)
        binding = ActivitySettingsBinding.inflate(layoutInflater) // for view
binding (b)
        val view = binding.root                          // for view binding (c)
        setContentView(view)                             // for view binding (d)
        val toolbar = binding.toolbar    //for initializing and binding the
toolbar
        setSupportActionBar(toolbar)

        if(savedInstanceState == null){
            supportFragmentManager
                .beginTransaction()
                .replace(R.id.preference_content, SettingsPreference()) //The
preference_content is located in activity_settings.xml while the
SettingsPreference is the class newly created below.
                .commit()
        }

        PreferenceManager.getDefaultSharedPreferences(this)
            .registerOnSharedPreferenceChangeListener(this)

        setUpToolbar() //This function is called to setup the toolbar
    }

    private fun setUpToolbar() {
        supportActionBar?.setDisplayHomeAsUpEnabled(true)
        supportActionBar?.setDisplayShowHomeEnabled(true)
```

```
        }

    class SettingsPreference: PreferenceFragmentCompat(){
        override fun onCreatePreferences(savedInstanceState: Bundle?,
rootKey: String?) {
            setPreferencesFromResource(R.xml.preference_settings, rootKey)
        }
    }

    override fun onSharedPreferenceChanged(sharedPreferences:
SharedPreferences?, key: String?) {

        }
    }
```

Commit changes

Now, we will commit the changes we have made at this stage.

Click the Commit tab below the Project tab on the left side of the window. Then, mark the "Default Changelist" and "Unversioned Files". Then, enter a commit message i.e. the description of the commit (e.g. "Commit done at Stage 27.") (above the commit button) > click "Commit".

In the dialog box for code analysis, showing info about the number of errors and warnings, ignore it and just click "Commit".

We now have all the files committed. Let us proceed by clicking the 'Project' tab above the 'Commit' tab.

Running the app

Also, at this stage, let us run the app in our emulator. We can click 'Settings' from the bottom navigation bar to see the progress we have made on adding the preferences to our Settings screen. Note that, we have not yet added functionalities to activate the switch for Home background and the preferences under Security section. We will do that in the next stage.

STAGE 28
Adding Functionality to some Settings Preferences

At this stage, we will be adding functionality to our switch preference with the key (key_gold_background) and the other preferences related to security category like key_password and key_security_question.

Activating the switchPreference

When the switchPreference with the key (key_gold_background) is switched on, we want the background color of the Home screen (which is a CoordinatorLayout in activity_main.xml) to be changed to my_gold_color (#B76E25).

Note that in activity_main.xml the CoordinatorLayout already has an Id of rvCoordinatorLayout which we earlier assigned to it. Also, colors.xml already has my_white and my_gold_color added in it.

Updating MainActivity

Inside our MainActivity.kt, we will declare a function named 'mySettings' and call it inside onCreate method

Now, let us declare the function as follows:

```kotlin
private fun mySettings(){
        val prefs =
PreferenceManager.getDefaultSharedPreferences(this)
        val keyGoldBackground =
prefs.getBoolean("key_gold_background", false) //the default
value is set to false.

// If the Home Background switch is ON, then the background
should be gold but if it is OFF, then
//the background should be white. As in the codes that follows.
        if (keyGoldBackground){

binding.rvCoordinatorLayout.setBackgroundColor(resources.getColor
(R.color.my_gold_color))
        }else{
binding.rvCoordinatorLayout.setBackgroundColor(resources.getColor
(R.color.my_white))
        }
    }
```

NB: Press Alt+Enter on PreferenceManager colored in red to import it.

Next, let us call the function inside onCreate method as follows:

```
mySettings()
```

Since our MainActivity and SearchResultActivity are using the same layout files, we will also define and call mySettings function in SearchResultActivity just as we have done in MainActivity.

Updating SearchResultActivity

Now, inside our SearchResultActivity.kt, we will enable the background of the Search screen to change when user switch-on Home Background.

So, we will also call mySettings() function inside onCreate method.

```
//Codes related to adding functionality to Switchpreference located in
the mySettings() function
        mySettings()
```

Next, let us declare the function below onCreate method.

```
    private fun mySettings() {
        val prefs =
PreferenceManager.getDefaultSharedPreferences(this)
        val keyGoldBackground =
prefs.getBoolean("key_gold_background", false) //the default value is
set to false.

// If the Home Background switch is ON, then the background should be
gold but if it is OFF, then
//the background should be white. As in the codes that follows.
        if (keyGoldBackground){
binding.rvCoordinatorLayout.setBackgroundColor(resources.getColor(R.co
lor.my_gold_color))
        }else{
binding.rvCoordinatorLayout.setBackgroundColor(resources.getColor(R.co
lor.my_white))
        }
    }
```

That's it for the switch preference.

Adding functionality to the Security-related preferences

When the preference for 'Require Password to open note' is enabled, we want a Toast message notifying the user to set a password and answer the security question to be shown on the settings screen, and also, we want the EditText view located in activity_entry.xml (with the id- edtPassword) for password entry to become visible in our EntryActivity. It should be visible only if the password has been set and the security question has been answered.

Once the field becomes visible, the note should open only after the correct password is entered in the text field. The password must be the same with the password that was set in the Settings screen for it to be recognized as correct password.

Now, let's get the work done.

Updating SettingsActivity.kt

Inside the onSharedPreferenceChanged method in our SettingsActivity, we need to enter some lines of code and update it as follows.

```kotlin
override fun onSharedPreferenceChanged(sharedPreferences: SharedPreferences?,
key: String?) {
    //The lines of code that follows will make a toast message to be
displayed when the preference to require password is enabled
    if(key=="key_secure"){
        val prefs = sharedPreferences?.getBoolean(key, false)
        when(prefs){
            true -> {
                Toast.makeText(this, getString(R.string.security_toast),
Toast.LENGTH_LONG).show()
            }
        }
    }
}
```

NB: For the string reference colored in red, we will have to update our strings.xml. This will be done as we proceed.

With that, a toast message will be shown to the user to set a password and answer the security question when the "Require Password to open note" is enabled.

Updating activity_entry.xml

In activity_entry.xml, we will add a new TextView named txvForgotPassword.

The TextView should be visible only if the user entered the wrong password 3 or 4 times. Also, a snackbar that will contain a message relating to the password hint should show.

So, let us add the textview as follows:

```xml
<TextView
    android:id="@+id/txvForgotPassword"
    android:layout_width="wrap_content"
    android:layout_height="wrap_content"
    android:layout_marginTop="8dp"
    android:backgroundTint="@color/my_white"
    android:text="@string/forgot_password_text"
    android:textColor="@color/black"
    android:textSize="16sp"
    android:visibility="invisible"
    android:textAlignment="center"
    app:layout_constraintEnd_toEndOf="parent"
    app:layout_constraintStart_toStartOf="parent"
    app:layout_constraintTop_toBottomOf="@+id/btnEntry" />
```

NB: For the string reference colored in red, we will update our strings.xml later.

Updating EntryActivity.kt

First, let us initialize and bind the EditText view for password entry (i.e. edtPassword) and the TextView for getting password hint (txvForgotPassword) as follows:

```kotlin
val edtPassword = binding.edtPassword    //for initializing and
binding the Password EditText view.
val txvForgotPassword = binding.txvForgotPassword    //for
initializing and binding the textview for getting password hint.
```

Next, let us enter the following lines of code still inside onCreate method.

So, we will declare a variable named prefs and store in it the values gotten from DefaultSharedPreferences of our PreferenceManager. We will then declare more immutable variable to get the values that have been indicated by the user.

That is,

```kotlin
val prefs = PreferenceManager.getDefaultSharedPreferences(this)
val keySecure = prefs.getBoolean("key_secure", false) //this get
the boolean value (true or false) indicated by user and sets the
default value to false.
val keyPassword = prefs.getString("key_password", "****")    //this
gets the password set by the user and sets a default value of
****
val keySecurityQuestion =
prefs.getString("key_security_question", "") //this gets the
answer the user provided for the security question.
```

130

Next, we will check to see if keySecure is set to true, that is, if "Require password to open note" is enabled. If it is checked, we will check if the user has entered a password and answered security question. If they have performed the two actions, then, the text field (edtPassword) for entering password should become visible, but if they have not performed any of the two actions, the edtPassword should remain invisible.

That is,

```
if (keySecure) {
    if(keyPassword.toString().isNotBlank() &&
        keyPassword.toString().isNotEmpty() &&
        keySecurityQuestion.toString().isNotBlank() &&
        keySecurityQuestion.toString().isNotEmpty()) {

        edtPassword.visibility = View.VISIBLE
    }
}
```

Next, we want to get the number of clicks on the "OPEN NOTE" button (btnEntry) and store it in a variable named countClick. So, let us declare the variable countClick and assign an initial value of 0 to it.

That is,

```
var clickCount = 0          //For initializing the number of clicks
on the 'open note' button to 0
```

Next, when the btnEntry button is clicked (that is, inside binding.btnEntry.setOnClickListener), we want the following actions to be performed.

First, the password entered by the user should be stored in a variable named "myPassword".

That is,

```
val myPassword = edtPassword.text.toString()
```

Second, the number of clicks should be incremented.

That is,

```
    clickCount++        //increment the number of clicks on "OPEN
NOTE" button.
```

Third, if the user should click the btnEntry three or four times consecutively, it is an indication that they have been entering wrong password, so, we want the hint in the text field for entering password to change to "Enter your password or best hobby", and the TextView that contains information about ForgotPassword should become visible, and at the same time, the softkeyboard should be hidden and a snackbar message showing password hint should be displayed for 7 seconds.

Also, but if the number of consecutive clicks is less than 3 or more than 4, the text view for ForgotPassword should be invisible and the hint in the EditText view (edtPassword) should be "Enter your password".

So, we will add the following lines of code:

```
binding.btnEntry.setOnClickListener {
    val myPassword = edtPassword.text.toString()

    clickCount++      //increment the number of clicks on "OPEN NOTE" button.

        if((clickCount == 3 || clickCount == 4) && myPassword !=
    keyPassword.toString().trim()){
            edtPassword.hint = getString(R.string.entry_hint_change) //
    change the hint in edtPassword to "Enter your password or best hobby"
            txvForgotPassword.visibility = View.VISIBLE

        /*Hide the keyboard after the text view for ForgotPassword is shown*/
        val hideKeyboard = getSystemService(Context.INPUT_METHOD_SERVICE) as
        InputMethodManager
        hideKeyboard.hideSoftInputFromWindow(txvForgotPassword.windowToken, 0 )

        Snackbar.make(
            view,
            getString(R.string.hint_part_a) + keyPassword.toString().length +
        getString(R.string.hint_part_b)     +
                getString(R.string.hint_part_c) +
        keyPassword.toString().first() + getString(R.string.hint_part_d) +
        keyPassword.toString().last(),
            Snackbar.LENGTH_INDEFINITE
        )
            .setDuration(7000)
            .show()

    }else{
        edtPassword.hint = getString(R.string.enter_your_password)
        txvForgotPassword.visibility = View.INVISIBLE
    }
```

Fourth, again if keySecure is true, that is, if the user has enabled "Require password to open note", we will check if the EditText view (edtPassword) for entering password is visible and then, we will change the password entered by the user, and the password and the security answer they already set from the Settings screen to lowercase, and then check if the password is the same with either the set password or the security answer. If they are the same, the note should open and then the password entered should be cleared.

That is,

```
if (keySecure) {
    if (edtPassword.isVisible &&
        myPassword.toLowerCase() ==
            keyPassword.toString().trim().toLowerCase() ||

        myPassword.toLowerCase() ==
            keySecurityQuestion.toString().trim().toLowerCase()) {

        val intent = Intent(this, MainActivity::class.java)
        startActivity(intent)
        edtPassword.text.clear()
```

Else, if the keySecure is true but the EditText view (edtPassword) is not visible, then, the note should open when btnEntry is clicked, but if the edtPassword is visible and the password does not match the values set at the Settings screen, then, a toast message notifying the user to enter the correct password should be displayed particularly if the number of clicks is not equal to 3 or 4.

That is,

```
    } else {
        if( edtPassword.visibility == View.GONE){
            val intent = Intent (this, MainActivity::class.java)
            startActivity(intent)
        }else {
            if(clickCount!=3 && clickCount!=4)
            Toast.makeText(
                this,
                getString(R.string.incorrect_password_toast),
                Toast.LENGTH_LONG
            ).show()
        }
    }
```

Nevertheless, if the keySecure is false; that is, the user has not enabled "Require password to open note", then, the EditText view (edtPassword) for password entry should not be visible and should not take up any space (that is, it should be set to GONE), and the note should open when btnEntry is clicked.

That is,

133

```
    }else{
        edtPassword.visibility = View.GONE
        val intent = Intent (this, MainActivity::class.java)
        startActivity(intent)
    }
```

So, in our EntryActivity.kt, we have:

```kotlin
package com.ajirelab.digitalnote

import android.content.Intent
import androidx.appcompat.app.AppCompatActivity
import android.os.Bundle
import android.view.View
import android.widget.Toast
import androidx.core.view.isVisible
import androidx.preference.PreferenceManager
import com.ajirelab.digitalnote.databinding.ActivityEntryBinding
import com.google.android.material.snackbar.Snackbar

class EntryActivity : AppCompatActivity() {
    private lateinit var binding: ActivityEntryBinding   // for view binding
(a)

    override fun onCreate(savedInstanceState: Bundle?) {
        super.onCreate(savedInstanceState)
        binding = ActivityEntryBinding.inflate(layoutInflater) // for view
binding (b)
        val view = binding.root                       // for view binding (c)
        setContentView(view)                          // for view binding (d)

        val edtPassword = binding.edtPassword      //for initializing and
binding the Password EditText view.
        val txvForgotPassword = binding.txvForgotPassword     //for
initializing and binding the textview for getting password hint.

        /*With these, when the users click the button_entry, they will be
redirected to MainActivity screen*/
        //If 'Require password to open note' is enabled in Settings screen, then
users will have to enter the password that they have set in order to open
note.

        val prefs = PreferenceManager.getDefaultSharedPreferences(this)

        val keySecure = prefs.getBoolean("key_secure", false) //this get the
boolean value (true or false) indicated by user and sets the default value to
false.
        val keyPassword = prefs.getString("key_password", "****")   //this
gets the password set by the user and sets a default value of ****
        val keySecurityQuestion = prefs.getString("key_security_question",
"") //this gets the answer the user provided for the security question.

// The text field for entering password (with the id edtPassword) should only
be visible
// if "Require Password to open note" (keySecure ) is enabled and the user
has entered password and answered security question.

        if (keySecure) {
```

```kotlin
        if(keyPassword.toString().isNotBlank() &&
            keyPassword.toString().isNotEmpty() &&
            keySecurityQuestion.toString().isNotBlank() &&
            keySecurityQuestion.toString().isNotEmpty()) {

            edtPassword.visibility = View.VISIBLE
        }
    }

    var clickCount = 0        //For initializing the number of clicks on
the 'open note' button to 0

// When the entry button is clicked, if the password entry field is visible
and the user has entered the correct password,
// the note should open, but if wrong password is entered, a toast message
should notify the user to enter the correct
// password.
// Also, if the keySecure is enabled, but the password entry field is not
visible because the user has not set a password
// and answered the security question, the note should still open when the
"open note" button is clicked.

    binding.btnEntry.setOnClickListener {
        val myPassword = edtPassword.text.toString()

        clickCount++        //increment the number of clicks on "OPEN
NOTE" button.
        if((clickCount == 3 || clickCount == 4) && myPassword !=
keyPassword.toString().trim()){
            edtPassword.hint = getString(R.string.entry_hint_change) //
change the hint in edtPassword to "Enter your password or best hobby"
            txvForgotPassword.visibility = View.VISIBLE

            Snackbar.make(
                view,
                getString(R.string.hint_part_a) +
keyPassword.toString().length + getString(R.string.hint_part_b)    +
                                getString(R.string.hint_part_c) +
keyPassword.toString().first() + getString(R.string.hint_part_d) +
keyPassword.toString().last(),
                Snackbar.LENGTH_INDEFINITE
            )
                .setDuration(7000)
                .show()

        }else{
            edtPassword.hint = getString(R.string.enter_your_password)
            txvForgotPassword.visibility = View.INVISIBLE
        }

        if (keySecure) {
            if (edtPassword.isVisible &&
                myPassword.toLowerCase() ==
keyPassword.toString().trim().toLowerCase() ||
                myPassword.toLowerCase() ==
keySecurityQuestion.toString().trim().toLowerCase()) {
                val intent = Intent(this, MainActivity::class.java)
                startActivity(intent)
                edtPassword.text.clear()
```

135

```
        } else {
            if( edtPassword.visibility == View.GONE){
                val intent = Intent (this, MainActivity::class.java)
                startActivity(intent)
            }else {
                if(clickCount!=3 && clickCount!=4)
                Toast.makeText(
                    this,
                    getString(R.string.incorrect_password_toast),
                    Toast.LENGTH_LONG
                ).show()
            }
        }
    }else{
        edtPassword.visibility = View.GONE
        val intent = Intent (this, MainActivity::class.java)
        startActivity(intent)
    }
    }
    }
}
```

NB: We are to press Alt+Enter on the following- that is, PreferenceManager, View, Toast, Invisible, Context, InputMethodManager- colored in red to import them.

Also, for the string reference colored in red, we will have to update our strings.xml file.

Updating strings.xml

We will need to add the following lines of code to update our strings.xml

```xml
<string name="incorrect_password_toast">Please enter the correct
password.</string>
<string name="security_toast">Set your password and answer the security
question.</string>
<string name="entry_hint_change">Enter your password or best hobby.</string>

<string name="forgot_password_toast">If you have forgotten your password,
enter the answer for the security question.</string>
<string name="forgot_password_text">Forgot Password? \n Enter the answer you
provided for security question \n OR \n Check the password hint in the
message below.</string>
<string name="hint_part_a">Your password has \u0020</string>
<string name="hint_part_b">\u0020 characters.\n</string>
<string name="hint_part_c"> It starts with \u0020</string>
<string name="hint_part_d"> \u0020 and ends with \u0020</string>
```

STAGE 29

Updating the MainActivity to exit when back is pressed (plus commit changes and app testing)

For the app to exit when the back button of the device is pressed, we have to override onBackPressed method and updated the code in it as follows:

```
/With the onBackPressed below, the app should exit when back is pressed from
the MainActivity.
    override fun onBackPressed() {
        super.onBackPressed()
        finishAffinity()
        finish()
    }
```

Commit changes

Now, we will commit the changes we have made at this stage.

Click the Commit tab below the Project tab on the left side of the window. Then, mark the "Default Changelist" and "Unversioned Files". Then, enter a commit message i.e. the description of the commit (e.g. "Commit done at Stage 29.") (above the commit button) >> click "Commit".

In the dialog box for code analysis, showing info about the number of errors and warnings, ignore it and just click "Commit".

We now have all the files committed. Let us now click the 'Project' tab above the 'Commit' tab.

Running the app

At this stage, let us run the app in our emulator. We can click 'Settings' and test the functionalities we have added to some of the settings preferences like the switch for Home background and the preferences under Security section.

STAGE 30
App Localization

In implementing localization, we will be adding French translation for the app.

First, we will check through our app to ensure that every word or string is changed to string resource and stored in strings.xml.

In the course of our coding, we have tried to ensure that all our strings are stored in strings.xml. However, if there is still any hardcoded text or word or statement that is yet to be changed to a string resource, we could change it as follows: place the mouse pointer on the hardcoded text, press Alt + Enter, then click "Extract String Resource" >> enter a resource name >> OK.

In short, all hardcoded texts should be changed to string resources inside strings.xml

In strings.xml, we now have:

```xml
<resources>
    <string name="app_name">Digital Note</string>

    <string name="action_settings">Settings</string>
    <string name="action_new_note">New Note</string>

    <string name="menu_home">Home</string>
    <string name="menu_settings">Settings</string>
    <string name="menu_search">Search</string>

    <string name="note_category">Note Category</string>
    <string name="note_title">Note Title</string>
    <string name="note_details">Note Details</string>

    <string name="cancel">Cancel</string>
    <string name="save">Save</string>

    <string name="note_saved">Note Saved Successfully.</string>
    <string name="note_updated">Note Updated.</string>
    <string name="note_deleted">Note Deleted.</string>
    <string name="not_saved">Not Saved.</string>

    <string name="open_note">Open Note</string>
    <string name="app_image_description">App logo description</string>
    <string name="enter_your_password">Enter your password</string>

    <string name="iv_content_description">Note image icon</string>
    <string name="ivdescription_delete_note">Note delete icon</string>
```

```xml
<string name="tv_last_updated_date">Last updated date.</string>

<string name="tv_date_created">Created date.</string>
<string name="time_last_updated">Last Updated:\u0020</string>

<string name="toast_you_are_here">You are here!</string>
<string name="confirm_note_delete">Are you sure you want to delete this note?</string>
<string name="yes">Yes</string>
<string name="no">No</string>

<string name="created">Created:\u0020</string>

<string name="search_note">Search</string>

<string name="prefcat_general">General</string>
<string name="swpref_summary">Change home background color to gold.</string>
<string name="swpref_title">Home Background</string>

<string name="prefcat_security">Security</string>
<string name="ckpref_security_title">Require password to open note.</string>
<string name="ckpref_security_summary">Set password and answer security question.</string>
<string name="edpref_title_password">Set a password</string>
<string name="edpref_default_password">****</string>
<string name="edpref_dialog_password">Change password</string>
<string name="edpref_title_question">Answer a security question</string>
<string name="edpref_dialog_question">What is your best hobby?</string>

<string name="prefcat_about">About</string>
<string name="pref_version">Version</string>
<string name="pref_version_summary">1.0 (Released: 2022)</string>
<string name="pref_developer">Developer</string>
<string name="pref_developer_summary">Joseph Ajireloja</string>
<string name="pref_storage_title">Storage</string>
<string name="pref_storage_summary">The notes are stored locally on device memory.</string>

<string name="settings">Settings</string>

<string name="incorrect_password_toast">Please enter the correct password.</string>
<string name="security_toast">Set your password and answer the security question.</string>
<string name="entry_hint_change">Enter your password or best hobby.</string>
<string name="forgot_password_toast">If you have forgotten your password, enter the answer to the security question.</string>
<string name="forgot_password_text">Forgot Password? \n Enter the answer you provided for security question \n OR \n Check the password
```

```
hint in the message below.</string>
    <string name="hint_part_a">Your password has \u0020</string>
    <string name="hint_part_b">\u0020 characters.\n</string>
    <string name="hint_part_c"> It starts with \u0020</string>
    <string name="hint_part_d"> \u0020 and ends with \u0020</string>
</resources>
```

Next, we will create a new android resource file for French language. To do this, we can follow the following procedure:

Right-click on "res" >> click "New" >> click "Android Resource File" >> From Available qualifier, select "Locale" and then click the forward arrow (>>). In Language, select "fr:French" >> under "Specific Region Only", select "Any Region". Now, Android Studio will automatically add "values-fr" as directory name >> For filename, enter "strings.xml" >> NB: Resource type = values and Root element = resources >> click OK (as in Figure 81).

In the prompt window that follows (if any), select YES.

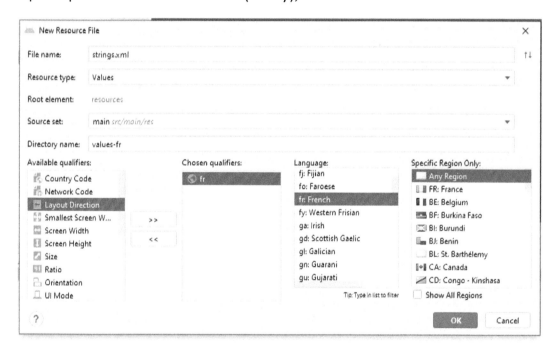

Figure 81

We now have fr/strings.xml.

Also, by default, we already have values/strings.xml in Android Studio.

Next, we will copy all the string resources from values/strings.xml and paste inside fr/strings.xml.

Now, in fr/strings.xml, we will change the English words in each of the string item to French words. *We could use www.deepl.com/translator and Google Translate (https://translate.google.com) to get the French translation for each word or statement. We could also seek the help of a native French speaker in vetting the translations that have been done.*

After the translation and modifications, **the content of fr/strings.xml is:**

```
<resources>
    <string name="app_name">Digital Note</string>
    <string name="action_settings">Paramètres</string>
    <string name="action_new_note">Nouvelle Note</string>

    <string name="menu_home">Accueil</string>
    <string name="menu_settings">Paramètres</string>
    <string name="menu_search">Chercher</string>

    <string name="note_category">Catégorie de note</string>
    <string name="note_title">Titre de la note</string>
    <string name="note_details">Détails de la note</string>

    <string name="cancel">Annuler</string>
    <string name="save">Sauvegarder</string>

    <string name="note_saved">Note Sauvegardée.</string>
    <string name="note_updated">Note mise à jour.</string>
    <string name="note_deleted">Note supprimée.</string>
    <string name="not_saved">Non Sauvegardé.</string>
    <string name="open_note">Note ouverte</string>
    <string name="app_image_description">Description du logo de
l\'application.</string>
    <string name="enter_your_password">Saisissez votre mot de
passe</string>

    <string name="iv_content_description">Icône de l\'image de la
note.</string>
    <string name="ivdescription_delete_note">Icône de suppression de
la note.</string>
    <string name="tv_last_updated_date">Date de la dernière mise à
jour.</string>

    <string name="tv_date_created">Date de création.</string>
    <string name="time_last_updated">Dernière mise a
jour:\u0020</string>

    <string name="toast_you_are_here">Vous êtes ici!</string>
    <string name="confirm_note_delete">Supprimer cette note?</string>
    <string name="yes">Oui</string>
    <string name="no">Non</string>

    <string name="created">Créé le:\u0020</string>
```

141

```xml
    <string name="search_note">Chercher</string>

    <string name="prefcat_general">Général</string>
    <string name="swpref_summary">Changer la couleur d\'arriere de la
page d\'accueil en or.</string>
    <string name="swpref_title">Fond de page d\'accueil</string>

    <string name="prefcat_security">Sécurité</string>
    <string name="ckpref_security_title">Exiger un mot de passe pour
ouvrir la note.</string>
    <string name="ckpref_security_summary">Définir le mot de passe et
répondre à la question de sécurité.</string>
    <string name="edpref_title_password">Définir un mot de
passe</string>
    <string name="edpref_default_password">****</string>
    <string name="edpref_dialog_password">Changer le mot de
passe</string>
    <string name="edpref_title_question">Répondre à une question de
sécurité</string>
    <string name="edpref_dialog_question">Quel est votre meilleur
passe-temps?</string>

    <string name="prefcat_about">À propos d\'app</string>
    <string name="pref_version">Version</string>
    <string name="pref_version_summary">1.0 (Publié : 2022)</string>
    <string name="pref_developer">Développeur</string>
    <string name="pref_developer_summary">Joseph Ajireloja</string>
    <string name="pref_storage_title">Stockage</string>
    <string name="pref_storage_summary">Les notes sont stockées
localement sur la mémoire de l\'appareil.</string>

    <string name="settings">Paramètres</string>

    <string name="incorrect_password_toast">Veuillez saisir le bon mot
de passe.</string>
    <string name="security_toast">Définissez votre mot de passe et
répondez à la question de sécurité.</string>
    <string name="entry_hint_change">Entrez votre mot de passe ou
votre meilleur passe-temps.</string>
    <string name="forgot_password_toast">Si vous avez oublié votre mot
de passe, entrez la réponse à la question de sécurité.</string>
    <string name="forgot_password_text">Mot de passe oublié? \n Entrez
la réponse que vous avez fournie pour la question de sécurité \n OU \n
Vérifiez l\'indice de mot de passe dans le message ci-
dessous.</string>
    <string name="hint_part_a">Votre mot de passe a \u0020</string>
    <string name="hint_part_b">\u0020 caractères.\n</string>
    <string name="hint_part_c">Cela commence par \u0020</string>
    <string name="hint_part_d">\u0020 et se termine par
\u0020</string>
</resources>
```

STAGE 31

Finishing Touches
(plus commit changes and generate APK)

Before generating the apk, let us do a slight modification to the content_note.xml by wrapping the TextInputLayout and the EditText for NoteDetails in a ScrollView. This will make the EditText view for entering the note details to be scrollable.

So, in the part for the Note Details, we now have:

```xml
<ScrollView
    android:id="@+id/layout_textNoteText"
    android:layout_width="0dp"
    android:layout_height="250dp"
    android:layout_marginTop="8dp"
    android:background="#EAE8E6"
    app:layout_constraintEnd_toEndOf="@+id/layout_textNoteTitle"
    app:layout_constraintStart_toStartOf="@+id/layout_textNoteTitle"
    app:layout_constraintTop_toBottomOf="@+id/layout_textNoteTitle">

    <com.google.android.material.textfield.TextInputLayout
        android:layout_width="match_parent"
        android:layout_height="wrap_content">

        <EditText
            android:id="@+id/textNoteText"
            android:layout_width="match_parent"
            android:layout_height="wrap_content"
            android:ems="10"
            android:gravity="start|top"
            android:hint="@string/note_details"
            android:inputType="textMultiLine"
            android:textSize="20sp" />

    </com.google.android.material.textfield.TextInputLayout>

</ScrollView>
```

Next, for Note Category and Note Title, we will change the textSize attribute to 18. Also, for Note Title alone, we will check to see that the maxLenght to 90.

Next, we will change the layout_marginTop of the 'cancel' and 'save' buttons to 12dp.

Updating AndroidManifest file

In addition, let us make one more modification. When we run the app, we will observe that the softKeyboard of the device covers the text being typed in the Note Detail's box. So, to address that, we will need to modify our AndroidManifest file by adding windowSoftInputMode attribute and setting its value to "adjustPan" in NoteActivity and EditNoteActivity tags.

That is,

```
<activity
    android:name=".EditNoteActivity"
    android:label="@string/note_details"
    android:windowSoftInputMode="adjustPan"/>

<activity
    android:name=".NoteActivity"
    android:label="@string/note_details"
    android:windowSoftInputMode="adjustPan"/>
```

Updating Module level build.gradle file- build.gradle (Module: Digital_Note.app)

Also, in the Module level gradle file, we will set minifyEnabled to true inside the release block. That is,

```
buildTypes {
    release {
        minifyEnabled true
```

Setting it to true will be of help when it's time to release or publish the app. It will enable ProGuard and make the app to be optimized and reduced in size.

That's all.

Now that we are done with the development of the app, we can generate its apk file and install it on our mobile device.

Commit changes

Let us commit the changes we have just made. We can enter "Commit done at Stage 31" as Commit message.

Generate APK

To generate apk for the app, we will go to Build menu >> then click 'Build Bundles / APK (s)' >> then, click 'Build APK(s)'.

You can send the APK file for the app to your mobile phone through USB cable or Xender or any other means.

In my own case, I sent the APK file to my mobile phone through Xender. To do this, open Xender application from your phone, go to the right Navigation menu icon and select 'Connect to PC', then, select the option to switch on your hotspot, turn on the Phone Hotspot; then, return to Xender. Notice the IP address that is now shown.

Go to your computer; from the Connection section at the bottom right, connect to the Hotspot of your phone. Next, open your web browser (e.g. Google Chrome) and enter the IP address (shown on your phone) into the address bar of your computer's web browser. Press 'Enter'. Your Phone's content or directories should now show on your computer. Next, locate the APK file generated from Android Studio and drap and drop it to the Phone screen on your web browser.

After the successful transfer of the apk file, you can then disconnect your phone from the computer. Next, locate the app from the Xender folder (e.g. inside 'Apps' folder or category on your phone.)

Next, Install the apk file, and then run the app.

The app should function as expected on the mobile phone.

APPENDIX
Compilation of All the Final Codes

build.gradle (Module: Digital_Note.app)

```
plugins {
    id 'com.android.application'
    id 'kotlin-android'
    id 'kotlin-kapt'
}

android {
    compileSdkVersion 31

    defaultConfig {
        applicationId "com.ajirelab.digitalnote"
        minSdkVersion 21
        targetSdkVersion 31
        versionCode 1
        versionName "1.0"

        testInstrumentationRunner "androidx.test.runner.AndroidJUnitRunner"
    }

    buildTypes {
        release {
            minifyEnabled true
            proguardFiles getDefaultProguardFile('proguard-android-
optimize.txt'), 'proguard-rules.pro'
        }
    }
    compileOptions {
        sourceCompatibility JavaVersion.VERSION_1_8
        targetCompatibility JavaVersion.VERSION_1_8
    }
    kotlinOptions {
        jvmTarget = '1.8'
    }
    buildFeatures {
        viewBinding = true
    }
}

dependencies {

    implementation "org.jetbrains.kotlin:kotlin-stdlib:$kotlin_version"
    implementation 'androidx.core:core-ktx:1.7.0'
    implementation 'androidx.appcompat:appcompat:1.4.1'
    implementation 'com.google.android.material:material:1.4.0'
    implementation 'androidx.constraintlayout:constraintlayout:2.1.3'
    testImplementation 'junit:junit:4.+'
    androidTestImplementation 'androidx.test.ext:junit:1.1.3'
    androidTestImplementation 'androidx.test.espresso:espresso-core:3.4.0'

    // Lifecycle dependencies
    def lifecycle_version = "2.4.0"
```

```
    implementation "androidx.lifecycle:lifecycle-viewmodel-
ktx:$lifecycle_version"
    implementation "androidx.lifecycle:lifecycle-livedata-
ktx:$lifecycle_version"
    implementation "androidx.lifecycle:lifecycle-common-
java8:$lifecycle_version"

    // Room dependencies
    def roomVersion = "2.3.0"
    implementation "androidx.room:room-runtime:$roomVersion"
    kapt "androidx.room:room-compiler:$roomVersion"
    androidTestImplementation "androidx.room:room-testing:$roomVersion"

    // For Preference library - Kotlin
    implementation 'androidx.preference:preference-ktx:1.1.1'

    //For Kotlin Coroutine
    implementation "androidx.room:room-ktx:$roomVersion"
    implementation 'org.jetbrains.kotlinx:kotlinx-coroutines-core:1.5.0'
    implementation 'org.jetbrains.kotlinx:kotlinx-coroutines-android:1.5.0'

}
```

build.gradle (Project: Digital_Note)

```
// Top-level build file where you can add configuration options common to all
sub-projects/modules.
buildscript {
    ext.kotlin_version = "1.4.31"
    repositories {
        google()
        mavenCentral()
    }
    dependencies {
        classpath "com.android.tools.build:gradle:4.2.0"
        classpath "org.jetbrains.kotlin:kotlin-gradle-plugin:$kotlin_version"

        // NOTE: Do not place your application dependencies here; they belong
        // in the individual module build.gradle files
    }
}

allprojects {
    repositories {
        google()
        mavenCentral()
        //jcenter() // Warning: this repository is going to shut down soon
    }
}
task clean(type: Delete) {
    delete rootProject.buildDir
}
```

gradle-wrapper.properties (Gradle Version)

```
#Sat Jan 15 11:45:14 WAT 2022
distributionBase=GRADLE_USER_HOME
```

```
distributionUrl=https\://services.gradle.org/distributions/gradle-6.7.1-
bin.zip
distributionPath=wrapper/dists
zipStorePath=wrapper/dists
zipStoreBase=GRADLE_USER_HOME
```

gradle.properties (Project Properties)

```
org.gradle.jvmargs=-Xmx2048m -Dfile.encoding=UTF-8
android.useAndroidX=true
android.enableJetifier=true
kotlin.code.style=official
```

settings.gradle (Project settings)

```
rootProject.name = "Digital Note"
include ':app'
```

local.properties (SDK location)

```
sdk.dir=C\:\\Users\\hp\\AppData\\Local\\Android\\Sdk
```

AndroidManifest.xml

```
<?xml version="1.0" encoding="utf-8"?>
<manifest xmlns:android="http://schemas.android.com/apk/res/android"
    package="com.ajirelab.digitalnote">

    <application
        android:allowBackup="true"
        android:icon="@drawable/my_app_icon"
        android:label="@string/app_name"
        android:roundIcon="@drawable/my_app_icon"
        android:supportsRtl="true"
        android:theme="@style/Theme.DigitalNote">

        <activity android:name=".SettingsActivity"
            android:label="@string/settings"
            android:parentActivityName=".MainActivity"/>

        <activity
            android:name=".SearchResultActivity"
            android:label="@string/search_note"
            android:parentActivityName=".MainActivity" />

        <activity
            android:name=".EditNoteActivity"
            android:label="@string/note_details"
            android:windowSoftInputMode="adjustPan"/>

        <activity
            android:name=".NoteActivity"
            android:label="@string/note_details"
            android:windowSoftInputMode="adjustPan"/>
```

```xml
        <activity
            android:name=".EntryActivity"
            android:exported="true">
            <intent-filter>
                <action android:name="android.intent.action.MAIN" />

                <category android:name="android.intent.category.LAUNCHER" />
            </intent-filter>
        </activity>
        <activity android:name=".MainActivity" />
    </application>

</manifest>
```

strings.xml

```xml
<resources>
    <string name="app_name">Digital Note</string>

    <string name="action_settings">Settings</string>
    <string name="action_new_note">New Note</string>

    <string name="menu_home">Home</string>
    <string name="menu_settings">Settings</string>
    <string name="menu_search">Search</string>

    <string name="note_category">Note Category</string>
    <string name="note_title">Note Title</string>
    <string name="note_details">Note Details</string>

    <string name="cancel">Cancel</string>
    <string name="save">Save</string>

    <string name="note_saved">Note Saved Successfully.</string>
    <string name="note_updated">Note Updated.</string>
    <string name="note_deleted">Note Deleted.</string>
    <string name="not_saved">Not Saved.</string>

    <string name="open_note">Open Note</string>
    <string name="app_image_description">App logo description</string>
    <string name="enter_your_password">Enter your password</string>

    <string name="iv_content_description">Note image icon</string>
    <string name="ivdescription_delete_note">Note delete icon</string>
    <string name="tv_last_updated_date">Last updated date.</string>

    <string name="tv_date_created">Created date.</string>
    <string name="time_last_updated">Last Updated:\u0020</string>

    <string name="toast_you_are_here">You are here!</string>
    <string name="confirm_note_delete">Are you sure you want to delete this
note?</string>
    <string name="yes">Yes</string>
    <string name="no">No</string>

    <string name="created">Created:\u0020</string>

    <string name="search_note">Search</string>
```

```xml
    <string name="prefcat_general">General</string>
    <string name="swpref_summary">Change home background color to
gold.</string>
    <string name="swpref_title">Home Background</string>

    <string name="prefcat_security">Security</string>
    <string name="ckpref_security_title">Require password to open
note.</string>
    <string name="ckpref_security_summary">Set password and answer security
question.</string>
    <string name="edpref_title_password">Set a password</string>
    <string name="edpref_default_password">****</string>
    <string name="edpref_dialog_password">Change password</string>
    <string name="edpref_title_question">Answer a security question</string>
    <string name="edpref_dialog_question">What is your best hobby?</string>


    <string name="prefcat_about">About</string>
    <string name="pref_version">Version</string>
    <string name="pref_version_summary">1.0 (Released: 2022)</string>
    <string name="pref_developer">Developer</string>
    <string name="pref_developer_summary">Joseph Ajireloja</string>
    <string name="pref_storage_title">Storage</string>
    <string name="pref_storage_summary">The notes are stored locally on
device memory.</string>

    <string name="settings">Settings</string>

    <string name="incorrect_password_toast">Please enter the correct
password.</string>
    <string name="security_toast">Set your password and answer the security
question.</string>
    <string name="entry_hint_change">Enter your password or best
hobby.</string>
    <string name="forgot_password_toast">If you have forgotten your password,
enter the answer to the security question.</string>
    <string name="forgot_password_text">Forgot Password? \n Enter the answer
you provided for security question \n OR \n Check the password hint in the
message below.</string>
    <string name="hint_part_a">Your password has \u0020</string>
    <string name="hint_part_b">\u0020 characters.\n</string>
    <string name="hint_part_c"> It starts with \u0020</string>
    <string name="hint_part_d"> \u0020 and ends with \u0020</string>

</resources>
```

strings.xml (fr)

```xml
<resources>
    <string name="app_name">Digital Note</string>

    <string name="action_settings">Paramètres</string>
    <string name="action_new_note">Nouvelle Note</string>

    <string name="menu_home">Accueil</string>
    <string name="menu_settings">Paramètres</string>
    <string name="menu_search">Chercher</string>
```

```xml
<string name="note_category">Catégorie de note</string>
<string name="note_title">Titre de la note</string>
<string name="note_details">Détails de la note</string>

<string name="cancel">Annuler</string>
<string name="save">Sauvegarder</string>

<string name="note_saved">Note Sauvegardée.</string>
<string name="note_updated">Note mise à jour.</string>
<string name="note_deleted">Note supprimée.</string>
<string name="not_saved">Non Sauvegardé.</string>

<string name="open_note">Note ouverte</string>
<string name="app_image_description">Description du logo de
l\'application.</string>
<string name="enter_your_password">Saisissez votre mot de passe</string>

<string name="iv_content_description">Icône de l\'image de la
note.</string>
<string name="ivdescription_delete_note">Icône de suppression de la
note.</string>
<string name="tv_last_updated_date">Date de la dernière mise à
jour.</string>

<string name="tv_date_created">Date de création.</string>
<string name="time_last_updated">Dernière mise a jour:\u0020</string>

<string name="toast_you_are_here">Vous êtes ici!</string>
<string name="confirm_note_delete">Supprimer cette note?</string>
<string name="yes">Oui</string>
<string name="no">Non</string>

<string name="created">Créé le:\u0020</string>

<string name="search_note">Chercher</string>

<string name="prefcat_general">Général</string>
<string name="swpref_summary">Changer la couleur d\'arriere de la page
d\'accueil en or.</string>
<string name="swpref_title">Fond de page d\'accueil</string>

<string name="prefcat_security">Sécurité</string>
<string name="ckpref_security_title">Exiger un mot de passe pour ouvrir
la note.</string>
<string name="ckpref_security_summary">Définir le mot de passe et
répondre à la question de sécurité.</string>
<string name="edpref_title_password">Définir un mot de passe</string>
<string name="edpref_default_password">****</string>
<string name="edpref_dialog_password">Changer le mot de passe</string>
<string name="edpref_title_question">Répondre à une question de
sécurité</string>
<string name="edpref_dialog_question">Quel est votre meilleur passe-
temps?</string>

<string name="prefcat_about">À propos d\'app</string>
<string name="pref_version">Version</string>
<string name="pref_version_summary">1.0 (Publié : 2022)</string>
<string name="pref_developer">Développeur</string>
<string name="pref_developer_summary">Joseph Ajireloja</string>
```

```xml
    <string name="pref_storage_title">Stockage</string>
    <string name="pref_storage_summary">Les notes sont stockées localement
sur la mémoire de l\'appareil.</string>

    <string name="settings">Paramètres</string>

    <string name="incorrect_password_toast">Veuillez saisir le bon mot de
passe.</string>
    <string name="security_toast">Définissez votre mot de passe et répondez à
la question de sécurité.</string>
    <string name="entry_hint_change">Entrez votre mot de passe ou votre
meilleur passe-temps.</string>
    <string name="forgot_password_toast">Si vous avez oublié votre mot de
passe, entrez la réponse à la question de sécurité.</string>
    <string name="forgot_password_text">Mot de passe oublié? \n Entrez la
réponse que vous avez fournie pour la question de sécurité \n OU \n Vérifiez
l\'indice de mot de passe dans le message ci-dessous.</string>
    <string name="hint_part_a">Votre mot de passe a \u0020</string>
    <string name="hint_part_b">\u0020 caractères.\n</string>
    <string name="hint_part_c">Cela commence par \u0020</string>
    <string name="hint_part_d">\u0020 et se termine par \u0020</string>

</resources>
```

colors.xml

```xml
<?xml version="1.0" encoding="utf-8"?>
<resources>
    <color name="purple_200">#FFBB86FC</color>
    <color name="purple_500">#FF6200EE</color>
    <color name="purple_700">#FF3700B3</color>
    <color name="teal_200">#FF03DAC5</color>
    <color name="teal_700">#FF018786</color>
    <color name="black">#FF000000</color>
    <color name="white">#FFFFFFFF</color>

    <!--    These are my custom colors -->
    <color name="my_primary_color">#F59707</color>
    <color name="my_primary_dark_color">#B75825</color>
    <color name="my_accent_color">#D81B60</color>
    <color name="my_light_green_color">#76BF5E</color>
    <color name="my_normal_green_color">#3F9224</color>
    <color name="my_gold_color">#B76E25</color>
    <color name="my_crimson_color">#DC143C</color>
    <color name="my_white">#FFFFFF</color>

</resources>
```

themes.xml

```xml
<resources xmlns:tools="http://schemas.android.com/tools">
    <!-- Base application theme. -->
    <style name="Theme.DigitalNote"
parent="Theme.MaterialComponents.DayNight.NoActionBar">
        <!-- Primary brand color. -->
        <item name="colorPrimary">@color/my_primary_color</item>
```

```xml
            <item name="colorPrimaryVariant">@color/my_primary_dark_color</item>
            <item name="colorOnPrimary">@color/white</item>
            <!-- Secondary brand color. -->
            <item name="colorSecondary">@color/my_accent_color</item>
            <item name="colorSecondaryVariant">@color/teal_700</item>
            <item name="colorOnSecondary">@color/black</item>

            <!-- Status bar color. -->
            <item name="android:statusBarColor"
tools:targetApi="l">?attr/colorPrimaryVariant</item>
            <!-- Customize your theme here. -->
    </style>
</resources>
```

themes.xml (night)

```xml
<resources xmlns:tools="http://schemas.android.com/tools">
    <!-- Base application theme. -->
    <style name="Theme.DigitalNote"
parent="Theme.MaterialComponents.DayNight.NoActionBar">
            <!-- Primary brand color. -->
            <item name="colorPrimary">@color/purple_200</item>
            <item name="colorPrimaryVariant">@color/my_primary_dark_color</item>
            <item name="colorOnPrimary">@color/black</item>
            <!-- Secondary brand color. -->
            <item name="colorSecondary">@color/my_accent_color</item>
            <item name="colorSecondaryVariant">@color/my_accent_color</item>
            <item name="colorOnSecondary">@color/black</item>

            <!-- Status bar color. -->
            <item name="android:statusBarColor"
tools:targetApi="l">?attr/colorPrimaryVariant</item>
            <!-- Customize your theme here. -->
    </style>
</resources>
```

menu.xml

```xml
<?xml version="1.0" encoding="utf-8"?>
<menu xmlns:android="http://schemas.android.com/apk/res/android"
    xmlns:app="http://schemas.android.com/apk/res-auto">
    <item
        android:id="@+id/action_new_note"
        android:orderInCategory="99"
        android:title="@string/action_new_note"
        app:showAsAction="never" />

    <item
        android:id="@+id/action_settings"
        android:orderInCategory="100"
        android:title="@string/action_settings"
        app:showAsAction="never" />
</menu>
```

153

bottom_navigation_menu.xml

```xml
<?xml version="1.0" encoding="utf-8"?>
<menu xmlns:android="http://schemas.android.com/apk/res/android">
    <item
        android:id="@+id/bottom_nav_home"
        android:icon="@drawable/ic_home"
        android:title="@string/menu_home" />

    <item
        android:id="@+id/bottom_nav_settings"
        android:icon="@drawable/ic_settings"
        android:title="@string/menu_settings" />

    <item
        android:id="@+id/bottom_nav_search"
        android:icon="@drawable/ic_search_black"
        android:title="@string/menu_search" />
</menu>
```

Drawables added:

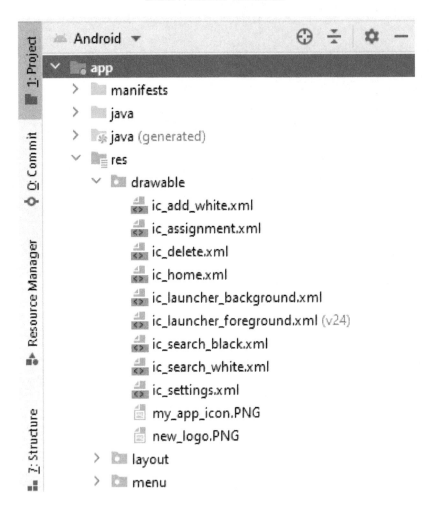

EntryActivity.kt

```kotlin
package com.ajirelab.digitalnote

import android.content.Context
import android.content.Intent
import androidx.appcompat.app.AppCompatActivity
import android.os.Bundle
import android.view.View
import android.view.inputmethod.InputMethodManager
import android.widget.Toast
import androidx.core.view.isVisible
import androidx.preference.PreferenceManager
import com.ajirelab.digitalnote.databinding.ActivityEntryBinding
import com.google.android.material.snackbar.Snackbar

class EntryActivity : AppCompatActivity() {
    private lateinit var binding: ActivityEntryBinding     // for view binding
(a)
```

```kotlin
    override fun onCreate(savedInstanceState: Bundle?) {
        super.onCreate(savedInstanceState)
        binding = ActivityEntryBinding.inflate(layoutInflater) // for view
binding (b)
        val view = binding.root                  // for view binding (c)
        setContentView(view)                     // for view binding (d)

        val edtPassword = binding.edtPassword    //for initializing and
binding the Password EditText view.
        val txvForgotPassword = binding.txvForgotPassword    //for
initializing and binding the textview for getting password hint.

        /*With these, when the users click the button_entry, they will be
redirected to MainActivity screen*/
//If 'Require password to open note' is enabled in Settings screen, then
users will have to enter the password that they have set in order to open
note.

        val prefs = PreferenceManager.getDefaultSharedPreferences(this)
        val keySecure = prefs.getBoolean("key_secure", false) //this get the
boolean value (true or false) indicated by user and sets the default value to
false.
        val keyPassword = prefs.getString("key_password", "****")    //this
gets the password set by the user and sets a default value of ****
        val keySecurityQuestion = prefs.getString("key_security_question",
"") //this gets the answer the user provided for the security question.

// The text field for entering password (with the id edtPassword) should only
be visible if "Require Password to open note" (keySecure ) is enabled and the
user has entered password and answered security question.

        if (keySecure) {
            if(keyPassword.toString().isNotBlank() &&
                keyPassword.toString().isNotEmpty() &&
                keySecurityQuestion.toString().isNotBlank() &&
                keySecurityQuestion.toString().isNotEmpty()) {

                edtPassword.visibility = View.VISIBLE
            }
        }

        var clickCount = 0        //For initializing the number of clicks on
the 'open note' button to 0

// When the entry button is clicked, if the password entry field is visible
and the user has entered the correct password,
// the note should open, but if wrong password is entered, a toast message
should notify the user to enter the correct password.
// Also, if the keySecure is enabled, but the password entry field is not
visible because the user has not set a password
// and answered the security question, the note should still open when the
"open note" button is clicked.

        binding.btnEntry.setOnClickListener {
            val myPassword = edtPassword.text.toString()

            clickCount++        //increment the number of clicks on "OPEN
NOTE" button.
            if((clickCount == 3 || clickCount == 4) && myPassword !=
```

```kotlin
keyPassword.toString().trim()){
                edtPassword.hint = getString(R.string.entry_hint_change) //
change the hint in edtPassword to "Enter your password or best hobby"
                txvForgotPassword.visibility = View.VISIBLE
        /*Hide the keyboard after the text view for ForgetPassword is shown*/
                val hideKeyboard =
getSystemService(Context.INPUT_METHOD_SERVICE) as InputMethodManager

hideKeyboard.hideSoftInputFromWindow(txvForgotPassword.windowToken, 0 )

                Snackbar.make(
                        view,
                        getString(R.string.hint_part_a) +
keyPassword.toString().length + getString(R.string.hint_part_b)    +
                            getString(R.string.hint_part_c) +
keyPassword.toString().first() + getString(R.string.hint_part_d) +
keyPassword.toString().last(),
                        Snackbar.LENGTH_INDEFINITE
                )
                        .setDuration(7000)
                        .show()

        }else{
            edtPassword.hint = getString(R.string.enter_your_password)
            txvForgotPassword.visibility = View.INVISIBLE
        }

        if (keySecure) {
            if (edtPassword.isVisible &&
                myPassword.toLowerCase() ==
keyPassword.toString().trim().toLowerCase() ||
                myPassword.toLowerCase() ==
keySecurityQuestion.toString().trim().toLowerCase()) {
                    val intent = Intent(this, MainActivity::class.java)
                    startActivity(intent)
                    edtPassword.text.clear()
            } else {
                if( edtPassword.visibility == View.GONE){
                    val intent = Intent (this, MainActivity::class.java)
                    startActivity(intent)
                }else {
                    if(clickCount!=3 && clickCount!=4)
                    Toast.makeText(
                        this,
                        getString(R.string.incorrect_password_toast),
                        Toast.LENGTH_LONG
                    ).show()
                }
            }
        }else{
            edtPassword.visibility = View.GONE
            val intent = Intent (this, MainActivity::class.java)
            startActivity(intent)
        }
    }
  }
}
```

activity_entry.xml

```xml
<?xml version="1.0" encoding="utf-8"?>
<androidx.constraintlayout.widget.ConstraintLayout
xmlns:android="http://schemas.android.com/apk/res/android"
    xmlns:app="http://schemas.android.com/apk/res-auto"
    xmlns:tools="http://schemas.android.com/tools"
    android:layout_width="match_parent"
    android:layout_height="match_parent"
    tools:context=".EntryActivity">

    <ImageView
        android:id="@+id/imageWelcome"
        android:layout_width="200dp"
        android:layout_height="200dp"
        android:layout_marginTop="50dp"
        android:contentDescription="@string/app_image_description"
        app:layout_constraintEnd_toEndOf="parent"
        app:layout_constraintStart_toStartOf="parent"
        app:layout_constraintTop_toTopOf="parent"
        app:srcCompat="@drawable/new_logo" />

    <EditText
        android:id="@+id/edtPassword"
        android:layout_width="0dp"
        android:layout_height="wrap_content"
        android:layout_marginStart="24dp"
        android:layout_marginTop="8dp"
        android:layout_marginEnd="24dp"
        android:ems="10"
        android:textSize="14sp"
        android:hint="@string/enter_your_password"
        android:inputType="textPassword"
        android:visibility="gone"
        app:layout_constraintEnd_toEndOf="parent"
        app:layout_constraintStart_toStartOf="parent"
        app:layout_constraintTop_toBottomOf="@+id/imageWelcome" />

    <Button
        android:id="@+id/btnEntry"
        android:layout_width="wrap_content"
        android:layout_height="wrap_content"
        android:layout_marginTop="8dp"
        android:backgroundTint="@color/my_primary_color"
        android:text="@string/open_note"
        android:textSize="20sp"
        app:layout_constraintEnd_toEndOf="parent"
        app:layout_constraintStart_toStartOf="parent"
        app:layout_constraintTop_toBottomOf="@+id/edtPassword" />

    <TextView
        android:id="@+id/txvForgotPassword"
        android:layout_width="wrap_content"
        android:layout_height="wrap_content"
        android:layout_marginTop="8dp"
        android:backgroundTint="@color/my_white"
        android:text="@string/forgot_password_text"
        android:textColor="@color/black"
        android:textSize="16sp"
```

```
            android:visibility="invisible"
            android:textAlignment="center"
            app:layout_constraintEnd_toEndOf="parent"
            app:layout_constraintStart_toStartOf="parent"
            app:layout_constraintTop_toBottomOf="@+id/btnEntry" />

</androidx.constraintlayout.widget.ConstraintLayout>
```

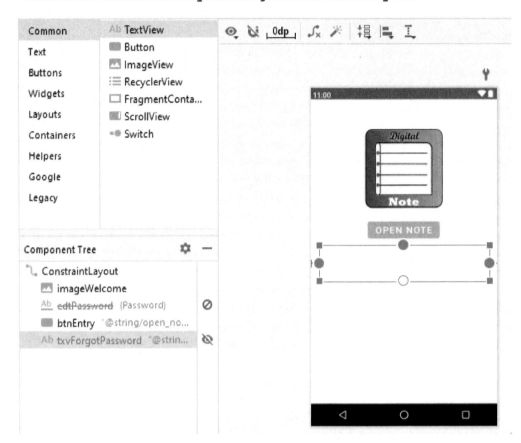

MainActivity.kt

```kotlin
package com.ajirelab.digitalnote

import android.app.Activity
import android.content.Intent
import androidx.appcompat.app.AppCompatActivity
import android.os.Bundle
import android.view.Menu
import android.view.MenuItem
import android.widget.Toast
import androidx.appcompat.app.AlertDialog
import androidx.lifecycle.Observer
import androidx.lifecycle.ViewModelProvider
import androidx.preference.PreferenceManager
import androidx.recyclerview.widget.LinearLayoutManager
import com.ajirelab.digitalnote.databinding.ActivityMainBinding
import java.util.*

class MainActivity : AppCompatActivity(),
```

159

```kotlin
NoteRecyclerAdapter.OnDeleteClickListener  {
    private lateinit var binding: ActivityMainBinding    // for view binding
(a)
    private lateinit var noteViewModel: NoteViewModel // for initializing the
ViewModel

    override fun onCreate(savedInstanceState: Bundle?) {
        super.onCreate(savedInstanceState)
        binding = ActivityMainBinding.inflate(layoutInflater) // for view
binding (b)
        val view = binding.root                    // for view binding (c)
        setContentView(view)                       // for view binding (d)

        val toolbar = binding.toolbar     //for initializing and binding the
toolbar
        val fab = binding.fab      ////for initializing and binding the
floating action button
        val bottomNavView = binding.bottomNavView  //for initializing and
binding the bottom navigation view

        val recyclerView = binding.layoutContentMain.noteItem  //for
initializing and binding the Recycler view
        setSupportActionBar(toolbar)

        mySettings()

        //Code for inflating the recyclerView using the RecyclerViewAdapter
        val noteRecyclerAdapter = NoteRecyclerAdapter(this, this)
        recyclerView.adapter = noteRecyclerAdapter

        //Code for adding layout Manager to the recycler View and making the
latest note to be on the top of the recyclerview.
        val myLayoutManager = LinearLayoutManager(this,
LinearLayoutManager.VERTICAL, true)
        myLayoutManager.stackFromEnd = true
        recyclerView.layoutManager = myLayoutManager

        fab.setOnClickListener {
            goToNewNote()
        }

        noteViewModel = ViewModelProvider(this,
ViewModelProvider.AndroidViewModelFactory.getInstance(application)).get(NoteV
iewModel::class.java)
        noteViewModel.allNotes.observe(this, Observer{notes ->
            notes?.let{
                noteRecyclerAdapter.setNotes(notes)
            }
        })

        bottomNavView.setOnItemSelectedListener {
            when(it.itemId) {
                R.id.bottom_nav_home ->
                    Toast.makeText(
                        applicationContext,
                        getString(R.string.toast_you_are_here),
                        Toast.LENGTH_SHORT
                    ).show()
```

```kotlin
                    R.id.bottom_nav_search -> goToSearchResultActivity()

                    R.id.bottom_nav_settings -> goToSettingsActivity()
                }
                true
            }
        }
    private fun mySettings(){
        val prefs = PreferenceManager.getDefaultSharedPreferences(this)
        val keyGoldBackground = prefs.getBoolean("key_gold_background",
false) //the default value is set to false.

// If the Home Background switch is ON, then the background should be gold
but if it is OFF, then
//the background should be white. As in the codes that follows.
        if (keyGoldBackground){

binding.rvCoordinatorLayout.setBackgroundColor(resources.getColor(R.color.my_
gold_color))
        }else{
binding.rvCoordinatorLayout.setBackgroundColor(resources.getColor(R.color.my_
white))
        }
    }

    private fun goToSearchResultActivity() {
        startActivity(Intent(this, SearchResultActivity::class.java))
    }

    private fun goToSettingsActivity() {
        startActivity(Intent(this, SettingsActivity::class.java))
    }

    override fun onCreateOptionsMenu(menu: Menu): Boolean {
        // Inflate the menu; this adds items to the action bar if it is
present.
        menuInflater.inflate(R.menu.menu, menu)
        return true
    }

    override fun onOptionsItemSelected(item: MenuItem): Boolean {
        if (item.itemId == R.id.action_settings){
            goToSettingsActivity()
        }

        if (item.itemId == R.id.action_new_note){
            goToNewNote()
        }
        return super.onOptionsItemSelected(item)
    }

    private fun goToNewNote() {
        val intent = Intent(this, NoteActivity::class.java)
        startActivityForResult(intent, NEW_NOTE_ACTIVITY_REQUEST_CODE)
    }

    override fun onActivityResult(requestCode: Int, resultCode: Int, data:
Intent?) {
        super.onActivityResult(requestCode, resultCode, data)
```

```kotlin
        if(requestCode == NEW_NOTE_ACTIVITY_REQUEST_CODE && resultCode ==
Activity.RESULT_OK) {
            val id = UUID.randomUUID().toString()
            val categoryName =
data?.getStringExtra(NoteActivity.NEW_CATEGORY)
            val titleName = data?.getStringExtra(NoteActivity.NEW_TITLE)
            val details = data?.getStringExtra(NoteActivity.NEW_DETAILS)
            val firstDate = data?.getStringExtra(NoteActivity.DATE_CREATED)
            val currentTime = Calendar.getInstance().time

            val note = Note(id, categoryName!!, titleName!!, details!!,
firstDate, currentTime)

            noteViewModel.insert(note)
            Toast.makeText(applicationContext, R.string.note_saved,
Toast.LENGTH_SHORT).show()

        } else if (requestCode == UPDATE_NOTE_ACTIVITY_REQUEST_CODE &&
resultCode == Activity.RESULT_OK) {
            val id = data?.getStringExtra(EditNoteActivity.ID)
            val categoryName =
data?.getStringExtra(EditNoteActivity.UPDATED_CATEGORY)
            val titleName =
data?.getStringExtra(EditNoteActivity.UPDATED_TITLE)
            val details =
data?.getStringExtra(EditNoteActivity.UPDATED_DETAILS)
            val firstDate = data?.getStringExtra(NoteActivity.DATE_CREATED)
            val currentTime = Calendar.getInstance().time

            val note = Note(id!!, categoryName!!, titleName!!, details!!,
firstDate, currentTime)

            //code to update
            noteViewModel.update(note)
            Toast.makeText(applicationContext, R.string.note_updated,
Toast.LENGTH_SHORT).show()

        }else{
            Toast.makeText(applicationContext, R.string.not_saved,
Toast.LENGTH_SHORT).show()
        }
    }

//Alert Dialog was activated to ensure that users confirm a note before
deletion
    override fun onDeleteClickListener(myNote: Note) {
        val builder = AlertDialog.Builder(this@MainActivity)
        builder.setMessage(getString(R.string.confirm_note_delete))
            .setCancelable(false)
            .setPositiveButton(getString(R.string.yes)) {
                dialog, id ->
                noteViewModel.delete(myNote)
                Toast.makeText(applicationContext, R.string.note_deleted,
Toast.LENGTH_SHORT).show()
            }
            .setNegativeButton(getString(R.string.no)) {
                dialog, id ->
                dialog.dismiss()
```

```kotlin
        }
        val alert = builder.create()
        alert.show()
    }

    override fun onResume() {
        super.onResume()
        val recyclerView = binding.layoutContentMain.noteItem  //for
initializing and binding the Recycler view
        recyclerView.adapter?.notifyDataSetChanged()
    }

    companion object{
        private const val NEW_NOTE_ACTIVITY_REQUEST_CODE = 1
        const val UPDATE_NOTE_ACTIVITY_REQUEST_CODE = 2
    }
//With the onBackPressed below, the app should exit when back is pressed from
the MainActivity.
    override fun onBackPressed() {
        super.onBackPressed()
        finishAffinity()
        finish()
    }
}
```

activity_main.xml

```xml
<?xml version="1.0" encoding="utf-8"?>
<androidx.constraintlayout.widget.ConstraintLayout
    xmlns:android="http://schemas.android.com/apk/res/android"
    xmlns:app="http://schemas.android.com/apk/res-auto"
    xmlns:tools="http://schemas.android.com/tools"
    android:layout_width="match_parent"
    android:layout_height="match_parent"
    tools:context=".MainActivity">

    <!--I added a coordinator layout inside which the AppBarLayout,
    the <include> element for the content_main.xml (which will contain the
recycler view) and the Floating Action Button were housed.-->

    <!-- I assigned an Id (rvCoordinatorLayout) and a background color to the
coordinatorlayout. These will be useful when it is time to change the
background color from Settings screen switch preference.-->

    <androidx.coordinatorlayout.widget.CoordinatorLayout
        android:layout_width="match_parent"
        android:layout_height="0dp"
        android:id="@+id/rvCoordinatorLayout"
        app:layout_constraintBottom_toTopOf="@+id/bottom_nav_view"
        app:layout_constraintEnd_toEndOf="parent"
        app:layout_constraintStart_toStartOf="parent"
        app:layout_constraintTop_toTopOf="parent"
        android:background="#FFFFFF"
        android:fitsSystemWindows="true">

        <com.google.android.material.appbar.AppBarLayout
          style="@style/Widget.MaterialComponents.AppBarLayout.PrimarySurface"
            android:layout_width="match_parent"
```

163

```xml
            android:layout_height="wrap_content"
            android:fitsSystemWindows="true">

        <com.google.android.material.appbar.MaterialToolbar
            android:id="@+id/toolbar"
          style="@style/Widget.MaterialComponents.Toolbar.PrimarySurface"
            android:layout_width="match_parent"
            android:layout_height="?attr/actionBarSize"
            android:elevation="4dp"
            app:layout_scrollFlags="scroll|enterAlways"/>

    </com.google.android.material.appbar.AppBarLayout>

    <include
        android:id="@+id/layout_content_main"
        layout="@layout/content_main" />

<com.google.android.material.floatingactionbutton.FloatingActionButton
        android:id="@+id/fab"
        android:layout_width="wrap_content"
        android:layout_height="wrap_content"
        android:layout_gravity="bottom|end"
        android:layout_margin="16dp"
        app:tint="@color/white"
        app:srcCompat="@drawable/ic_add_white" />

    </androidx.coordinatorlayout.widget.CoordinatorLayout>

    <!--Also, I referenced the bottom_navigation_menu in the
BottomNavigationView I added.-->

    <com.google.android.material.bottomnavigation.BottomNavigationView
        android:id="@+id/bottom_nav_view"
        android:layout_width="match_parent"
        android:layout_height="wrap_content"
        app:layout_constraintBottom_toBottomOf="parent"
        app:layout_constraintEnd_toEndOf="parent"
        app:layout_constraintStart_toStartOf="parent"
        app:menu="@menu/bottom_navigation_menu" />

</androidx.constraintlayout.widget.ConstraintLayout>
```

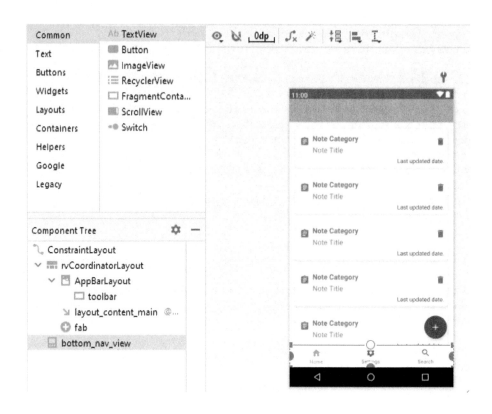

content_main.xml

```xml
<?xml version="1.0" encoding="utf-8"?>
<androidx.constraintlayout.widget.ConstraintLayout
    xmlns:android="http://schemas.android.com/apk/res/android"
    xmlns:app="http://schemas.android.com/apk/res-auto"
    xmlns:tools="http://schemas.android.com/tools"
    android:layout_width="match_parent"
    android:layout_height="match_parent"
    app:layout_behavior="@string/appbar_scrolling_view_behavior"
    tools:context=".MainActivity"
    tools:showIn="@layout/activity_main">

    <androidx.recyclerview.widget.RecyclerView
        android:id="@+id/noteItem"
        android:layout_width="0dp"
        android:layout_height="0dp"
        android:layout_margin="8dp"
        app:layout_constraintBottom_toBottomOf="parent"
        app:layout_constraintStart_toStartOf="parent"
        app:layout_constraintEnd_toEndOf="parent"
        app:layout_constraintTop_toTopOf="parent"
        tools:listitem="@layout/item_note_list"/>

</androidx.constraintlayout.widget.ConstraintLayout>
```

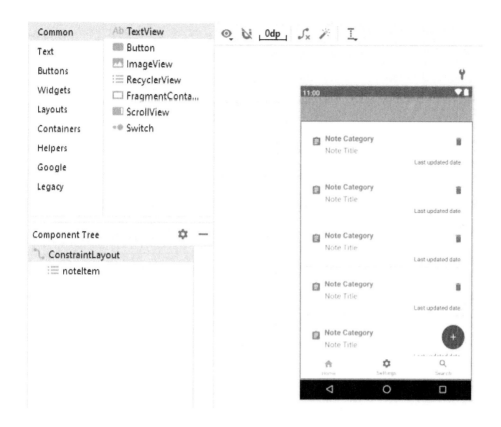

item_note_list.xml

```xml
<?xml version="1.0" encoding="utf-8"?>
<FrameLayout xmlns:android="http://schemas.android.com/apk/res/android"
    xmlns:app="http://schemas.android.com/apk/res-auto"
    android:layout_width="match_parent"
    android:layout_height="wrap_content">

    <androidx.cardview.widget.CardView
        android:layout_width="match_parent"
        android:layout_height="wrap_content"
        app:cardCornerRadius="6dp"
        app:cardElevation="4dp"
        app:cardUseCompatPadding="true"
        app:contentPadding="4dp">

        <androidx.constraintlayout.widget.ConstraintLayout
            android:layout_width="match_parent"
            android:layout_height="wrap_content">

            <ImageView
                android:id="@+id/ivCardImage"
                android:layout_width="wrap_content"
                android:layout_height="wrap_content"
                android:layout_marginStart="8dp"
                android:layout_marginTop="16dp"
                android:tint="@color/my_gold_color"
                app:layout_constraintStart_toStartOf="parent"
                app:layout_constraintTop_toTopOf="parent"
                app:srcCompat="@drawable/ic_assignment"
```

166

```xml
            android:contentDescription="@string/iv_content_description"
    />
            <TextView
                android:id="@+id/tvNoteCategory"
                android:layout_width="0dp"
                android:layout_height="wrap_content"
                android:layout_marginStart="8dp"
                android:layout_marginTop="8dp"
                android:layout_marginEnd="16dp"
                android:text="@string/note_category"

              android:textAppearance="@style/TextAppearance.AppCompat.Medium"
                android:textColor="@color/my_gold_color"
                android:textStyle="bold"
                app:layout_constraintEnd_toStartOf="@+id/ivDelete"
                app:layout_constraintStart_toEndOf="@id/ivCardImage"
                app:layout_constraintTop_toTopOf="parent" />

            <TextView
                android:id="@+id/tvNoteTitle"
                android:layout_width="0dp"
                android:layout_height="wrap_content"
                android:layout_marginStart="8dp"
                android:layout_marginTop="5dp"
                android:layout_marginEnd="16dp"
                android:text="@string/note_title"
              android:textAppearance="@style/TextAppearance.AppCompat.Medium"
                android:textSize="18sp"
                app:layout_constraintEnd_toStartOf="@+id/ivDelete"
                app:layout_constraintStart_toEndOf="@id/ivCardImage"
                app:layout_constraintTop_toBottomOf="@id/tvNoteCategory" />

            <ImageView
                android:id="@+id/ivDelete"
                android:layout_width="wrap_content"
                android:layout_height="wrap_content"
                android:layout_marginTop="16dp"
                android:layout_marginEnd="2dp"
                app:layout_constraintEnd_toEndOf="parent"
                app:layout_constraintTop_toTopOf="parent"
                app:srcCompat="@drawable/ic_delete"
            android:contentDescription="@string/ivdescription_delete_note" />

            <TextView
                android:id="@+id/tvLastUpdated"
                android:layout_width="wrap_content"
                android:layout_height="wrap_content"
                android:layout_marginTop="4dp"
                android:layout_marginEnd="4dp"
                android:layout_marginBottom="4dp"
                android:text="@string/tv_last_updated_date"
                android:textColor="@color/my_accent_color"
                app:layout_constraintBottom_toBottomOf="parent"
                app:layout_constraintEnd_toEndOf="parent"
                app:layout_constraintTop_toBottomOf="@+id/tvNoteTitle" />

        </androidx.constraintlayout.widget.ConstraintLayout>
    </androidx.cardview.widget.CardView>
</FrameLayout>
```

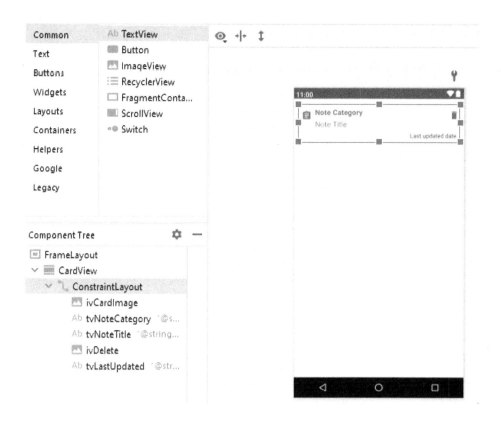

NoteActivity.kt

```kotlin
package com.ajirelab.digitalnote

import android.app.Activity
import android.content.Intent
import androidx.appcompat.app.AppCompatActivity
import android.os.Bundle
import android.view.View
import com.ajirelab.digitalnote.databinding.ActivityNoteBinding
import java.text.SimpleDateFormat
import java.util.*

class NoteActivity : AppCompatActivity() {
    private lateinit var binding: ActivityNoteBinding    // for view binding
for activity_note (a)

    override fun onCreate(savedInstanceState: Bundle?) {
        super.onCreate(savedInstanceState)

        binding = ActivityNoteBinding.inflate(layoutInflater)    // for view
binding for activity note (b)
        val view = binding.root                        // for view binding (c)
        setContentView(view)                           // for view binding (d)

        val toolbar = binding.toolbar
        setSupportActionBar(toolbar)
```

```kotlin
        val buttonSave = binding.layoutContentNote.buttonSave           //for
initializing and binding save button
        val buttonCancel = binding.layoutContentNote.buttonCancel
//for initializing and binding cancel button
        val txvLastUpdated = binding.layoutContentNote.txvLastUpdated    //for
initializing and binding last updated textview
        val txvDateCreated = binding.layoutContentNote.txvDateCreated   //for
initializing and binding date created textview

//NB: The layoutContentNote was formed by default from the id (i.e.
layout_content_note)that I assigned to the include tag for content_note.xml

        txvLastUpdated.visibility = View.INVISIBLE

        //For the purpose of formatting date created.
        val dateTime: String
        val calendar : Calendar = Calendar.getInstance()
        val simpleDateFormat = SimpleDateFormat("dd-MM-yyyy",
Locale.getDefault())
        dateTime = simpleDateFormat.format(calendar.time).toString()
        txvDateCreated.text = getString(R.string.created) + dateTime

        buttonSave.setOnClickListener {
            saveNote()
            finish()
        }

        buttonCancel.setOnClickListener {
            finish()
        }
    }

    //Note will also be saved when the back button of the device is pressed.
    override fun onBackPressed() {
        saveNote()
        super.onBackPressed()
    }

    private fun saveNote(){
        val resultIntent = Intent()
        if (binding.layoutContentNote.textNoteTitle.text.toString().trim() ==
"" &&
            binding.layoutContentNote.textNoteText.text.toString().trim() ==
"" ){
            setResult(Activity.RESULT_CANCELED, resultIntent)
        }else{
            val category =
binding.layoutContentNote.noteCategory.text.toString()
            val title =
binding.layoutContentNote.textNoteTitle.text.toString()
            val details =
binding.layoutContentNote.textNoteText.text.toString()
            val firstDate =
binding.layoutContentNote.txvDateCreated.text.toString()

            resultIntent.putExtra(NEW_CATEGORY, category)
            resultIntent.putExtra(NEW_TITLE, title)
            resultIntent.putExtra(NEW_DETAILS, details)
            resultIntent.putExtra(DATE_CREATED, firstDate)
```

```
                setResult(Activity.RESULT_OK, resultIntent)
        }
    }

    companion object{
        const val NEW_CATEGORY - "new_category"
        const val NEW_TITLE = "new_title"
        const val NEW_DETAILS ="new_details"
        const val DATE_CREATED = "date_created"


    }
}
```

EditNoteActivity.kt

```
package com.ajirelab.digitalnote

import android.app.Activity
import android.content.Intent
import androidx.appcompat.app.AppCompatActivity
import android.os.Bundle
import com.ajirelab.digitalnote.databinding.ActivityNoteBinding


class EditNoteActivity : AppCompatActivity() {

    var id: String? = null

    private lateinit var binding: ActivityNoteBinding   // for view binding
for activity_note (a)

    override fun onCreate(savedInstanceState: Bundle?) {
        super.onCreate(savedInstanceState)

        binding =
            ActivityNoteBinding.inflate(layoutInflater)   // for view binding
for activity_note (b)
        val view = binding.root                 // for view binding (c)
        setContentView(view)                    // for view binding (d)

        val toolbar = binding.toolbar
        setSupportActionBar(toolbar)

        val noteCategory =
            binding.layoutContentNote.noteCategory        //for
initializing and binding note category
        val textNoteTitle =
            binding.layoutContentNote.textNoteTitle       //for
initializing and binding note title
        val textNoteText =
            binding.layoutContentNote.textNoteText        //for
initializing and binding note text
        val buttonSave =
            binding.layoutContentNote.buttonSave        //for initializing
and binding save button
        val buttonCancel =
            binding.layoutContentNote.buttonCancel        //for
initializing and binding cancel button
        val txvLastUpdated =
```
170

```kotlin
        binding.layoutContentNote.txvLastUpdated    //for initializing and
binding last updated textview
        val txvDateCreated =
            binding.layoutContentNote.txvDateCreated    //for initializing and
binding date created textview

//NB: The layoutContentNote was formed by default from the id (i.e.
layout_content_note) that I assigned to the include tag for content_note.xml

        val bundle: Bundle? = intent.extras
        bundle?.let {
            id = bundle.getString("id")
            val title = bundle.getString("title")
            val category = bundle.getString("category")
            val details = bundle.getString("details")
            val dateCreated = bundle.getString("dateCreated")
            val lastUpdated = bundle.getString("lastUpdated")

            noteCategory.setText(category)
            textNoteTitle.setText(title)
            textNoteText.setText(details)
            txvDateCreated.text = dateCreated
            txvLastUpdated.text = lastUpdated

            buttonSave.setOnClickListener {
                updateNote()
                finish()
            }

            buttonCancel.setOnClickListener {
                finish()
            }
        }
    }

//Note will also be updated when the back button of the device is pressed.
    override fun onBackPressed() {
        updateNote()
        super.onBackPressed()
    }

    private fun updateNote(){
        val updatedCategory =
binding.layoutContentNote.noteCategory.text.toString()
        val updatedTitle =
binding.layoutContentNote.textNoteTitle.text.toString()
        val updatedDetails =
binding.layoutContentNote.textNoteText.text.toString()
        val dateCreated =
binding.layoutContentNote.txvDateCreated.text.toString()

        val resultIntent = Intent()
        resultIntent.putExtra(ID, id)
        resultIntent.putExtra(UPDATED_CATEGORY, updatedCategory)
        resultIntent.putExtra(UPDATED_TITLE, updatedTitle)
        resultIntent.putExtra(UPDATED_DETAILS, updatedDetails)
        resultIntent.putExtra(DATE_CREATED, dateCreated)
        setResult(Activity.RESULT_OK, resultIntent)
    }
```

```
    companion object{
        const val ID = "note_id"
        const val UPDATED_CATEGORY = "category_name"
        const val UPDATED_TITLE = "title_name"
        const val UPDATED_DETAILS = "details"
        const val DATE_CREATED = "date_created"
    }
}
```

activity_note.xml

```xml
<?xml version="1.0" encoding="utf-8"?>
<androidx.coordinatorlayout.widget.CoordinatorLayout
    xmlns:android="http://schemas.android.com/apk/res/android"
    xmlns:app="http://schemas.android.com/apk/res-auto"
    xmlns:tools="http://schemas.android.com/tools"
    android:layout_width="match_parent"
    android:layout_height="match_parent"
    tools:context=".NoteActivity">

    <!-- For App Bar layout-->
    <com.google.android.material.appbar.AppBarLayout
        style="@style/Widget.MaterialComponents.AppBarLayout.PrimarySurface"
        android:layout_width="match_parent"
        android:layout_height="wrap_content"
        android:fitsSystemWindows="true">

        <com.google.android.material.appbar.MaterialToolbar
            android:id="@+id/toolbar"
            style="@style/Widget.MaterialComponents.Toolbar.PrimarySurface"
            android:layout_width="match_parent"
            android:layout_height="?attr/actionBarSize"
            android:elevation="4dp"
            app:layout_scrollFlags="scroll|enterAlways"/>

    </com.google.android.material.appbar.AppBarLayout>

    <include
        android:id="@+id/layout_content_note"
        layout="@layout/content_note" />

</androidx.coordinatorlayout.widget.CoordinatorLayout>
```

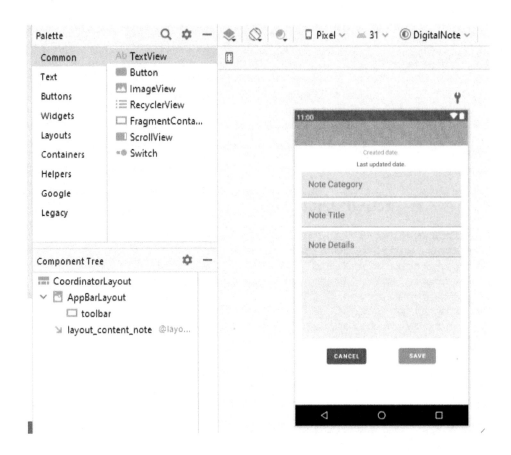

content_note.xml

```xml
<?xml version="1.0" encoding="utf-8"?>
<androidx.constraintlayout.widget.ConstraintLayout
xmlns:android="http://schemas.android.com/apk/res/android"
    android:layout_width="match_parent"
    android:layout_height="match_parent"
    xmlns:app="http://schemas.android.com/apk/res-auto"
    xmlns:tools="http://schemas.android.com/tools"
    app:layout_behavior="@string/appbar_scrolling_view_behavior"
    tools:showIn="@layout/activity_note">
    <!--    The app:layout_behavior="@string/appbar_scrolling_view_behavior"
    and tools:showIn="@layout/activity_note" above makes the Action bar to
show properly.
    Also, it makes the actionbar to be appropriately positioned in
activity_note.xml-->

    <TextView
        android:id="@+id/txvDateCreated"
        android:layout_width="wrap_content"
        android:layout_height="wrap_content"
        android:layout_marginStart="16dp"
        android:layout_marginTop="6dp"
        android:layout_marginEnd="16dp"
        android:text="@string/tv_date_created"
        android:textColor="@color/my_normal_green_color"
        app:layout_constraintEnd_toEndOf="parent"
        app:layout_constraintStart_toStartOf="parent"
        app:layout_constraintTop_toTopOf="parent" />
```

```xml
<TextView
    android:id="@+id/txvLastUpdated"
    android:layout_width="0dp"
    android:layout_height="wrap_content"
    android:layout_marginStart="16dp"
    android:layout_marginTop="8dp"
    android:layout_marginEnd="16dp"
    android:text="@string/tv_last_updated_date"
    android:textAlignment="center"
    android:textColor="@color/my_accent_color"
    app:layout_constraintEnd_toEndOf="parent"
    app:layout_constraintStart_toStartOf="parent"
    app:layout_constraintTop_toBottomOf="@id/txvDateCreated" />

<com.google.android.material.textfield.TextInputLayout
    android:layout_width="match_parent"
    android:layout_height="wrap_content"
    android:id="@+id/layout_noteCategory"
    android:layout_marginStart="16dp"
    android:layout_marginTop="8dp"
    android:layout_marginEnd="16dp"
    app:layout_constraintEnd_toEndOf="parent"
    app:layout_constraintStart_toStartOf="parent"
    app:layout_constraintTop_toBottomOf="@+id/txvLastUpdated">

    <EditText
        android:id="@+id/noteCategory"
        android:layout_width="match_parent"
        android:layout_height="wrap_content"
        android:hint="@string/note_category"
        android:textSize="18sp"
        android:inputType="textMultiLine"
        android:maxLength="50"/>
</com.google.android.material.textfield.TextInputLayout>

<com.google.android.material.textfield.TextInputLayout
    android:layout_width="0dp"
    android:layout_height="wrap_content"
    android:id="@+id/layout_textNoteTitle"
    android:layout_marginTop="8dp"
    app:layout_constraintEnd_toEndOf="@+id/layout_noteCategory"
    app:layout_constraintStart_toStartOf="@+id/layout_noteCategory"
    app:layout_constraintTop_toBottomOf="@+id/layout_noteCategory">

    <EditText
        android:id="@+id/textNoteTitle"
        android:layout_width="match_parent"
        android:layout_height="wrap_content"
        android:ems="10"
        android:maxLength="90"
        android:gravity="start|top"
        android:hint="@string/note_title"
        android:inputType="textMultiLine"
        android:textSize="18sp"/>
</com.google.android.material.textfield.TextInputLayout>

<ScrollView
    android:id="@+id/layout_textNoteText"
```

174

```
            android:layout_width="0dp"
            android:layout_height="245dp"
            android:layout_marginTop="8dp"
            android:background="#EAE8E6"
            app:layout_constraintEnd_toEndOf="@+id/layout_textNoteTitle"
            app:layout_constraintStart_toStartOf="@+id/layout_textNoteTitle"
            app:layout_constraintTop_toBottomOf="@+id/layout_textNoteTitle">

            <com.google.android.material.textfield.TextInputLayout
                android:layout_width="match_parent"
                android:layout_height="wrap_content">

                <EditText
                    android:id="@+id/textNoteText"
                    android:layout_width="match_parent"
                    android:layout_height="wrap_content"
                    android:ems="10"
                    android:gravity="start|top"
                    android:hint="@string/note_details"
                    android:inputType="textMultiLine"
                    android:textSize="18sp" />

            </com.google.android.material.textfield.TextInputLayout>
    </ScrollView>

    <Button
        android:id="@+id/buttonCancel"
        android:layout_width="wrap_content"
        android:layout_height="wrap_content"
        android:layout_marginStart="16dp"
        android:layout_marginTop="12dp"
        android:layout_marginEnd="8dp"
        android:text="@string/cancel"
        android:textStyle="bold"
        android:backgroundTint="@color/my_crimson_color"
        app:layout_constraintEnd_toStartOf="@+id/buttonSave"
        app:layout_constraintHorizontal_bias="0.5"
        app:layout_constraintStart_toStartOf="parent"
        app:layout_constraintTop_toBottomOf="@+id/layout_textNoteText" />

    <Button
        android:id="@+id/buttonSave"
        android:layout_width="wrap_content"
        android:layout_height="wrap_content"
        android:layout_marginStart="8dp"
        android:layout_marginTop="12dp"
        android:layout_marginEnd="16dp"
        android:text="@string/save"
        android:backgroundTint="@color/my_normal_green_color"
        android:textStyle="bold"
        app:layout_constraintEnd_toEndOf="parent"
        app:layout_constraintHorizontal_bias="0.5"
        app:layout_constraintStart_toEndOf="@+id/buttonCancel"
        app:layout_constraintTop_toBottomOf="@+id/layout_textNoteText" />

</androidx.constraintlayout.widget.ConstraintLayout>
```

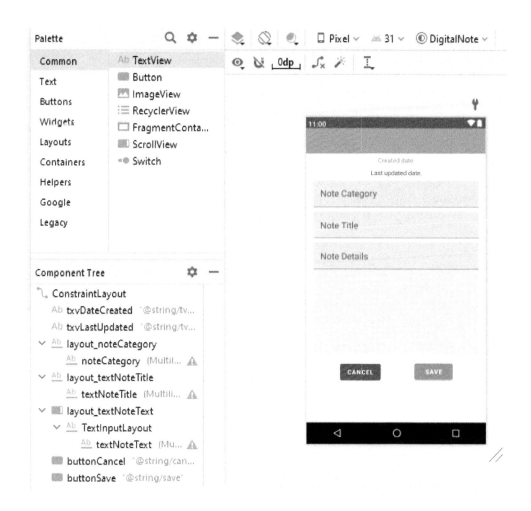

SettingsActivity.kt

```kotlin
package com.ajirelab.digitalnote

import android.content.SharedPreferences
import androidx.appcompat.app.AppCompatActivity
import android.os.Bundle
import android.widget.Toast
import androidx.preference.PreferenceFragmentCompat
import androidx.preference.PreferenceManager
import com.ajirelab.digitalnote.databinding.ActivitySettingsBinding

class SettingsActivity : AppCompatActivity(),
SharedPreferences.OnSharedPreferenceChangeListener {
    private lateinit var binding: ActivitySettingsBinding    // for view
binding (a)

    override fun onCreate(savedInstanceState: Bundle?) {
        super.onCreate(savedInstanceState)
        binding = ActivitySettingsBinding.inflate(layoutInflater) // for view
binding (b)
        val view = binding.root                        // for view binding (c)
        setContentView(view)                           // for view binding (d)
        val toolbar = binding.toolbar    //for initializing and binding the
toolbar

        setSupportActionBar(toolbar)
```

```kotlin
        if(savedInstanceState == null){
            supportFragmentManager
                .beginTransaction()
                .replace(R.id.preference_content, SettingsPreference()) //The
preference_content is located in activity_settings.xml while the
SettingsPreference is the class newly created below.
                .commit()
        }

        PreferenceManager.getDefaultSharedPreferences(this)
            .registerOnSharedPreferenceChangeListener(this)

        setUpToolbar() //This function is called to setup the toolbar

    }

    private fun setUpToolbar() {
        supportActionBar?.setDisplayHomeAsUpEnabled(true)
        supportActionBar?.setDisplayShowHomeEnabled(true)
    }

    class SettingsPreference: PreferenceFragmentCompat(){
        override fun onCreatePreferences(savedInstanceState: Bundle?,
rootKey: String?) {
            setPreferencesFromResource(R.xml.preference_settings, rootKey)
        }
    }

    override fun onSharedPreferenceChanged(sharedPreferences:
SharedPreferences?, key: String?) {
        //The lines of code that follows will make a toast message to be
displayed when the preference to require password is enabled
        if(key=="key_secure"){
            val prefs = sharedPreferences?.getBoolean(key, false)
            when(prefs){
                true -> {
                    Toast.makeText(this, getString(R.string.security_toast),
Toast.LENGTH_LONG).show()
                }
            }
        }
    }
}
```

activity_settings.xml

```xml
<?xml version="1.0" encoding="utf-8"?>
<androidx.constraintlayout.widget.ConstraintLayout
xmlns:android="http://schemas.android.com/apk/res/android"
    xmlns:app="http://schemas.android.com/apk/res-auto"
    xmlns:tools="http://schemas.android.com/tools"
    android:layout_width="match_parent"
    android:layout_height="match_parent"
    tools:context=".SettingsActivity">
    <!--    This is the code for adding the toolbar app action bar to the
activity. -->
    <com.google.android.material.appbar.AppBarLayout
        style="@style/Widget.MaterialComponents.AppBarLayout.PrimarySurface"
```

```
        android:id="@+id/appBarLayout"
        android:layout_width="match_parent"
        android:layout_height="wrap_content"
        app:layout_constraintTop_toTopOf="parent"
        app:layout_constraintEnd_toEndOf="parent"
        app:layout_constraintStart_toStartOf="parent"
        android:fitsSystemWindows="true">

        <com.google.android.material.appbar.MaterialToolbar
            android:id="@+id/toolbar"
            style="@style/Widget.MaterialComponents.Toolbar.PrimarySurface"
            android:layout_width="match_parent"
            android:layout_height="?attr/actionBarSize"
            android:elevation="4dp"
            app:layout_scrollFlags="scroll|enterAlways"/>

    </com.google.android.material.appbar.AppBarLayout>

    <FrameLayout
        android:id="@+id/preference_content"
        android:layout_width="match_parent"
        android:layout_height="0dp"
        app:layout_constraintBottom_toBottomOf="parent"
        app:layout_constraintEnd_toEndOf="parent"
        app:layout_constraintStart_toStartOf="parent"
        app:layout_constraintTop_toBottomOf="@id/appBarLayout">
    </FrameLayout>

</androidx.constraintlayout.widget.ConstraintLayout>
```

preference_settings.xml (in values > xml)

```xml
<?xml version="1.0" encoding="utf-8"?>
<PreferenceScreen xmlns:android="http://schemas.android.com/apk/res/android"
    xmlns:app="http://schemas.android.com/apk/res-auto">

    <PreferenceCategory
        android:title="@string/prefcat_general"
        app:iconSpaceReserved="false">

        <SwitchPreferenceCompat
            android:defaultValue="false"
            android:key="key_gold_background"
            android:summary="@string/swpref_summary"
            android:title="@string/swpref_title"
            app:iconSpaceReserved="false" />

    </PreferenceCategory>

    <PreferenceCategory
        android:title="@string/prefcat_security"
        app:iconSpaceReserved="false">

        <CheckBoxPreference
            android:defaultValue="false"
            android:key="key_secure"
            android:title="@string/ckpref_security_title"
            android:summaryOn="@string/ckpref_security_summary"
            app:iconSpaceReserved="false" />

<!--android:summaryOn attribute makes the summary to show only when the box
is checked-->

        <EditTextPreference
            android:dependency="key_secure"
            android:defaultValue="@string/edpref_default_password"
            android:dialogTitle="@string/edpref_dialog_password"
            android:key="key_password"
            android:title="@string/edpref_title_password"
            app:iconSpaceReserved="false"
            android:inputType="textPassword"
            android:imeOptions="flagNoExtractUi"/>
<!--     android:dependency attribute makes the preference to be activated
only if key_secure is enabled.
android:imeOptions="flagNoExtractUi".  with this, the orientation change will
not affect the password-type display.-->

        <EditTextPreference
            android:dependency="key_secure"
            android:defaultValue=""
            android:dialogTitle="@string/edpref_dialog_question"
            android:key="key_security_question"
            android:title="@string/edpref_title_question"
            app:iconSpaceReserved="false"
            android:inputType="textPassword"
            android:imeOptions="flagNoExtractUi"/>
<!--     android:imeOptions="flagNoExtractUi".  with this, the orientation
change will not affect the password-type display. -->
```

```
    </PreferenceCategory>

    <PreferenceCategory
        android:title="@string/prefcat_about"
        app:iconSpaceReserved="false">

        <Preference
            android:key="key_version"
            android:summary="@string/pref_version_summary"
            android:title="@string/pref_version"
            app:iconSpaceReserved="false" />

        <Preference
            android:key="key_developer"
            android:title="@string/pref_developer"
            android:summary="@string/pref_developer_summary"
            app:iconSpaceReserved="false"/>

        <Preference
            android:key="key_storage"
            android:title="@string/pref_storage_title"
            android:summary="@string/pref_storage_summary"
            app:iconSpaceReserved="false"/>

    </PreferenceCategory>

</PreferenceScreen>
```

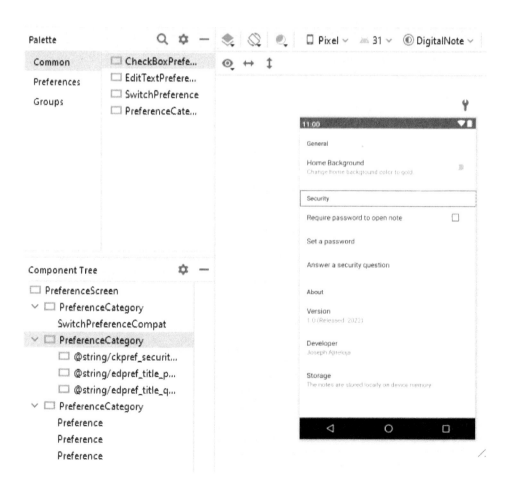

SearchResultActivity.kt

```kotlin
package com.ajirelab.digitalnote

import android.app.Activity
import android.content.Intent
import androidx.appcompat.app.AppCompatActivity
import android.os.Bundle
import android.view.Menu
import android.view.View
import android.widget.Toast
import androidx.appcompat.app.AlertDialog
import androidx.lifecycle.Observer
import androidx.lifecycle.ViewModelProvider
import androidx.preference.PreferenceManager
import androidx.recyclerview.widget.LinearLayoutManager
import com.ajirelab.digitalnote.databinding.ActivityMainBinding
import java.util.*


class SearchResultActivity : AppCompatActivity(),
NoteRecyclerAdapter.OnDeleteClickListener  {

    private lateinit var binding: ActivityMainBinding     // for view binding
initialization(a)
    private lateinit var searchViewModel: SearchViewModel     //Code for
initializing the search view model (a)
    private var noteRecyclerAdapter: NoteRecyclerAdapter? = null     //for
recordRecyclerAdapter (a) we initialized it and set its value to null.

    override fun onCreate(savedInstanceState: Bundle?) {
        super.onCreate(savedInstanceState)
        binding = ActivityMainBinding.inflate(layoutInflater)     // for view
binding (b)
        val view = binding.root                        // for view binding (c)
        setContentView(view)                       // for view binding (d)

        val toolbar = binding.toolbar     //for initializing and binding the
toolbar
        val fab = binding.fab     ////for initializing and binding the
floating action button
        val bottomNavView = binding.bottomNavView     //for initializing and
binding the bottom navigation view

        val recyclerView = binding.layoutContentMain.noteItem     //for
initializing and binding the Recycler view

        setSupportActionBar(toolbar)
        supportActionBar?.setDisplayHomeAsUpEnabled(true)     //This makes the
back icon to show on the Action bar

        //Codes related to adding functionality to Switchpreference located
in the mySettings() function
        mySettings()

        //Code for inflating the recyclerView using the RecyclerViewAdapter
        noteRecyclerAdapter = NoteRecyclerAdapter(this, this)     //for
```

```kotlin
noteRecyclerAdapter (b)
        recyclerView.adapter = noteRecyclerAdapter

        //Code for adding layout Manager to the recycler View and making the
latest note to be on the top of the recyclerview
        val myLayoutManager = LinearLayoutManager(this,
LinearLayoutManager.VERTICAL, true)
        myLayoutManager.stackFromEnd = true
        recyclerView.layoutManager = myLayoutManager

        fab.visibility = View.INVISIBLE    // this was added to make the fab
button in activity_main.xml invisible in SearchResultActivity
        bottomNavView.visibility = View.GONE // this was added to make the
bottom navigation bar in activity_main.xml invisible and without taking any
space in SearchResultActivity

        //code for initializing the searchViewModel   (b)
        searchViewModel = ViewModelProvider(this,

ViewModelProvider.AndroidViewModelFactory.getInstance(application)).get(Searc
hViewModel::class.java
        )
    }

    private fun mySettings() {
        val prefs = PreferenceManager.getDefaultSharedPreferences(this)
        val keyGoldBackground = prefs.getBoolean("key_gold_background",
false) //the default value is set to false.


// If the Home Background switch is ON, then the background should be gold
but if it is OFF, then the background should be white. As in the codes that
follows.
        if (keyGoldBackground){

binding.rvCoordinatorLayout.setBackgroundColor(resources.getColor(R.color.my_
gold_color))
        }else{
binding.rvCoordinatorLayout.setBackgroundColor(resources.getColor(R.color.my_
white))
        }
    }

    override fun onCreateOptionsMenu(menu: Menu): Boolean {
        // Inflate the menu; this adds items to the action bar  and then
activates the search menu to work
        menuInflater.inflate(R.menu.search_menu, menu)
        val search = menu.findItem(R.id.searchItems)
        val searchView = search.actionView as
androidx.appcompat.widget.SearchView
        searchView.isSubmitButtonEnabled = true

        //After entering the line next to this comment, I pressed Alt + Enter
on 'object' and then selected to implement its members.
        //Then, the onQueryTextSubmit and onQueryTextChange overrides were
added. I then added some codes into them.
        searchView.setOnQueryTextListener(object :
androidx.appcompat.widget.SearchView.OnQueryTextListener{
            override fun onQueryTextSubmit(query: String?): Boolean {
```

```
            if (query != null){
                getItemsFromDb(query)
            }
            return true
        }

        override fun onQueryTextChange(newText: String?): Boolean {
            if (newText != null){
                getItemsFromDb(newText)
            }
            return true
        }
    })
    return true
}
```

//The getItemFromDb function below was called inside the onCreateOptionsmenu above. The function is part of the code to handle the search functionality

```
private fun getItemsFromDb(searchText: String) {
    var searchText = searchText
    searchText = "%$searchText%"
    searchViewModel.searchForItems(desc = searchText)?.observe(this,
Observer {notes ->
        notes?.let { noteRecyclerAdapter!!.setNotes(notes) }
    })
}
```

// The codes below are to handle the updating of the notes directly from this SearchResultActivity.
```
override fun onActivityResult(requestCode: Int, resultCode: Int, data:
Intent?) {
    super.onActivityResult(requestCode, resultCode, data)
    if (requestCode == UPDATE_NOTE_ACTIVITY_REQUEST_CODE && resultCode ==
Activity.RESULT_OK) {
        val id = data?.getStringExtra(EditNoteActivity.ID)
        val categoryName =
data?.getStringExtra(EditNoteActivity.UPDATED_CATEGORY)
        val titleName =
data?.getStringExtra(EditNoteActivity.UPDATED_TITLE)
        val details =
data?.getStringExtra(EditNoteActivity.UPDATED_DETAILS)
        val firstDate = data?.getStringExtra(NoteActivity.DATE_CREATED)
        val currentTime = Calendar.getInstance().time

        val note = Note(id!!, categoryName!!, titleName!!, details!!,
firstDate, currentTime)

        //code to update
        searchViewModel.update(note)
        Toast.makeText(applicationContext, R.string.note_updated,
Toast.LENGTH_SHORT).show()

    }else{
        Toast.makeText(applicationContext, R.string.not_saved,
Toast.LENGTH_SHORT).show()
    }
}
```

```kotlin
    //The codes in the onDeleteClickListener below handles the deletion of
notes right from the SearchResultActivity
    //Alert Dialog was activated to ensure that users confirm a record before
deletion
    override fun onDeleteClickListener(myNote: Note) {
        val builder = AlertDialog.Builder(this)
        builder.setMessage(getString(R.string.confirm_note_delete))
            .setCancelable(false)
            .setPositiveButton(getString(R.string.yes)) {
                    dialog, id ->
                searchViewModel.delete(myNote)
                Toast.makeText(applicationContext, R.string.note_deleted,
Toast.LENGTH_SHORT).show()
            }
            .setNegativeButton(getString(R.string.no)) {
                    dialog, id ->
                dialog.dismiss()
            }
        val alert = builder.create()
        alert.show()
    }

    companion object{
        const val UPDATE_NOTE_ACTIVITY_REQUEST_CODE = 2
    }
}
```

search_menu.xml

```xml
<?xml version="1.0" encoding="utf-8"?>
<menu xmlns:android="http://schemas.android.com/apk/res/android"
    xmlns:app="http://schemas.android.com/apk/res-auto">
    <item android:id="@+id/searchItems"
        android:title="Search"
        android:icon="@drawable/ic_search_white"
        app:showAsAction="ifRoom"
        app:actionViewClass="androidx.appcompat.widget.SearchView"/>
</menu>
```

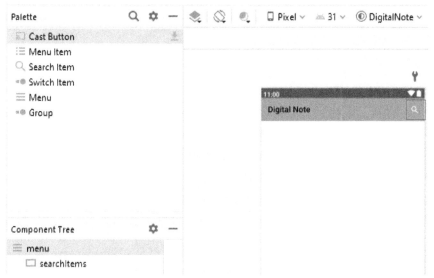

NoteViewModel.kt

```kotlin
package com.ajirelab.digitalnote

import android.app.Application
import androidx.lifecycle.AndroidViewModel
import androidx.lifecycle.LiveData
import androidx.lifecycle.viewModelScope
import kotlinx.coroutines.*

class NoteViewModel(application: Application): AndroidViewModel(application)
{

    val allNotes: LiveData<List<Note>>
    val noteRepository: NoteRepository

    init {
        val dao = NoteRoomDatabase.getDatabase(application)!!.noteDao()
        noteRepository = NoteRepository(dao)
        allNotes = noteRepository.allNotes
    }

    fun insert(note: Note) = viewModelScope.launch(Dispatchers.IO) {
        noteRepository.insert(note)
    }

    fun update(note: Note) = viewModelScope.launch(Dispatchers.IO){
        noteRepository.update(note)
    }

    fun delete(note: Note) = viewModelScope.launch(Dispatchers.IO) {
        noteRepository.delete(note)
    }
}
```

SearchViewModel.kt

```kotlin
package com.ajirelab.digitalnote

import android.app.Application
import androidx.lifecycle.AndroidViewModel
import androidx.lifecycle.LiveData
import androidx.lifecycle.viewModelScope
import kotlinx.coroutines.Dispatchers
import kotlinx.coroutines.launch

class SearchViewModel(application: Application):
AndroidViewModel(application) {


    val allNotes: LiveData<List<Note>>
    val noteRepository: NoteRepository

    init {
        val dao = NoteRoomDatabase.getDatabase(application)!!.noteDao()
```

```kotlin
        noteRepository = NoteRepository(dao)
        allNotes = noteRepository.allNotes
    }

    fun update(note: Note) = viewModelScope.launch(Dispatchers.IO){
        noteRepository.update(note)
    }

    fun delete(note: Note) = viewModelScope.launch(Dispatchers.IO) {
        noteRepository.delete(note)
    }

    fun searchForItems(desc: String) : LiveData<List<Note>>?{
        return noteRepository.search(desc)
    }
}
```

Note.kt

```kotlin
package com.ajirelab.digitalnote

import androidx.room.ColumnInfo
import androidx.room.Entity
import androidx.room.PrimaryKey
import java.util.*

@Entity (tableName = "notes")
class Note (@PrimaryKey
            val id: String,

            val category: String,

            val title: String,

            val details: String,

            @ColumnInfo(name = "date_created")
            val dateCreated: String?,

            @ColumnInfo(name = "last_updated")
            val lastUpdated: Date?)
```

NoteDao.kt

```kotlin
package com.ajirelab.digitalnote

import androidx.lifecycle.LiveData
import androidx.room.*

@Dao
interface NoteDao {
    @Insert
    suspend fun insert(note: Note)

    @get:Query("SELECT * FROM notes")
    val allNotes: LiveData<List<Note>>
```

```
//     //The next two lines implemented search query. NB: title, category and
details are from Note.kt
    @Query("SELECT * FROM notes WHERE title LIKE :desc OR category LIKE :desc
OR details LIKE :desc")
    fun getSearchResults(desc: String): LiveData<List<Note>>

    @Update
    suspend fun update(note: Note)

    @Delete
    suspend fun delete(note: Note)


}

//NB: We used suspend fun because we will be using it with Coroutines.
//We will also use the suspend fun in our NoteRepository.
```

NoteRepository.kt

```
package com.ajirelab.digitalnote

import androidx.annotation.WorkerThread
import androidx.lifecycle.LiveData

class NoteRepository(private val noteDao: NoteDao) {

    val allNotes: LiveData<List<Note>> = noteDao.allNotes

    //The next two lines are for implementing the search functionality
    @WorkerThread
    fun search(desc: String): LiveData<List<Note>>?{
        return noteDao.getSearchResults(desc)
    }

    suspend fun insert(note: Note) {
        noteDao.insert(note)
    }

    suspend fun update(note: Note){
        noteDao.update(note)
    }

    suspend fun delete(note: Note){
        noteDao.delete(note)
    }
}

//NB: We used suspend fun because we will be using it with Coroutines.
//We have also used the suspend fun in our NoteDao.kt.
```

DateTypeConverter.kt

```
package com.ajirelab.digitalnote

import androidx.room.TypeConverter
```

```kotlin
import java.util.*

class DateTypeConverter {
    @TypeConverter
    fun toDate(value: Long?): Date? {
        return if(value == null) null else Date(value)
    }

    @TypeConverter
    fun toLong(value: Date?): Long? {
        return value?.time
    }
}
```

NoteRoomDatabase.kt

```kotlin
package com.ajirelab.digitalnote

import android.content.Context
import androidx.room.Database
import androidx.room.Room
import androidx.room.RoomDatabase
import androidx.room.TypeConverters

@Database(entities = [Note::class], version = 1, exportSchema = false)
@TypeConverters(DateTypeConverter::class)

abstract class NoteRoomDatabase: RoomDatabase() {

    abstract fun noteDao(): NoteDao

    companion object{
        private var noteRoomInstance: NoteRoomDatabase? = null
        fun getDatabase(context: Context): NoteRoomDatabase?{
            if (noteRoomInstance == null) {
                synchronized(NoteRoomDatabase::class.java){
                    if (noteRoomInstance == null){
                        noteRoomInstance =
Room.databaseBuilder(context.applicationContext,
                        NoteRoomDatabase::class.java,
"note_database").build()
                    }
                }
            }
            return noteRoomInstance
        }
    }
}
```

NoteRecyclerAdapter.kt

```kotlin
package com.ajirelab.digitalnote

import android.app.Activity
import android.content.Context
import android.content.Intent
```

```kotlin
import android.view.LayoutInflater
import android.view.ViewGroup
import androidx.recyclerview.widget.RecyclerView
import com.ajirelab.digitalnote.databinding.ItemNoteListBinding
import java.text.SimpleDateFormat
import java.util.*

class NoteRecyclerAdapter(private val context: Context,
                          private val onDeleteClickListener:
OnDeleteClickListener) :
RecyclerView.Adapter<NoteRecyclerAdapter.NoteViewHolder>() {

    interface OnDeleteClickListener {
        fun onDeleteClickListener(myNote: Note)
    }

    private var noteList: List<Note> = mutableListOf()

    override fun onCreateViewHolder(parent: ViewGroup, viewType: Int):
NoteViewHolder {
        val binding =
ItemNoteListBinding.inflate(LayoutInflater.from(parent.context), parent,
false)
        return NoteViewHolder(binding)
    }

    override fun onBindViewHolder(holder: NoteViewHolder, position: Int) {
        val note = noteList[position]
        holder.setData(note.category, note.title, note.lastUpdated, position)
        holder.setListeners()
    }

    override fun getItemCount(): Int = noteList.size

    fun setNotes(notes: List<Note>) {
        noteList = notes
        notifyDataSetChanged()
    }

    inner class NoteViewHolder(val binding: ItemNoteListBinding) :
RecyclerView.ViewHolder(binding.root) {
        private var pos: Int = 0

        fun setData(category: String, title : String, lastUpdated: Date?,
position: Int) {
            binding.tvNoteCategory.text = category
            binding.tvNoteTitle.text = title
            binding.tvLastUpdated.text = getFormattedDate(lastUpdated)

            this.pos = position
        }

        private fun getFormattedDate(lastUpdated: Date?): String {
            var time = context.getString(R.string.time_last_updated)
            time += lastUpdated?.let {
                val sdf = SimpleDateFormat("HH:mm d MMM, yyyy",
Locale.getDefault())
                sdf.format(lastUpdated)
            } ?: "Not found"
```

189

```
            return time
        }

    fun setListeners() {
        itemView.setOnClickListener {
            val intent = Intent(context, EditNoteActivity::class.java)
            intent.putExtra("id", noteList[pos].id)
            intent.putExtra("category", noteList[pos].category)
            intent.putExtra("title", noteList[pos].title)
            intent.putExtra("details", noteList[pos].details)
            intent.putExtra("dateCreated", noteList[pos].dateCreated)
            intent.putExtra("lastUpdated",
getFormattedDate(noteList[pos].lastUpdated))
            (context as Activity).startActivityForResult(intent,
MainActivity.UPDATE_NOTE_ACTIVITY_REQUEST_CODE)
        }

        binding.ivDelete.setOnClickListener {
            onDeleteClickListener.onDeleteClickListener(noteList[pos])
        }
    }

    }
}
```

That's all about all the lines of code that make up the app.

The short link of the address of the website designed for the app is **bit.ly/digital-note**.

THANK YOU.

I WISH YOU THE BEST IN YOUR ANDROID APPLICATION DEVELOPMENT PRACTICES.

Printed in Great Britain
by Amazon

22509777R00110